# Tropical Freshwater Aquaria

George Cust & Peter Bird

illustrated by George Thompson

**Hamlyn**
London · New York · Sydney · Toronto

# FOREWORD

The hobby of tropical fish keeping has much to recommend it. Tropical fishes are clean, do not smell, do not need letting out at night and can be left for up to three weeks while their owner is away on holiday. The well-kept community tank is also a decorative feature which is an asset to any home.

This book is a short guide written to help the beginner avoid those elementary mistakes which so easily occur and which can be so discouraging. However, we have attempted to deal with the subject in a scientific manner, to provide a background for understanding the biology of tropical fishes and to serve as an introduction for further reading. In the study of tropical fishes there are still more questions unanswered than facts known, so even novice aquarists with time, interest and patience can make completely new observations and valuable contributions to our biological knowledge.

We would like to thank the curators of various Aquaria throughout the world for their assistance with this book. We would like particularly to thank our colleagues in the British Aquarist Study Society who have supplied us with much valuable information, comments and suggestions.

G.C.
P.B.

Published by The Hamlyn Publishing Group Limited
London · New York · Sydney · Toronto
Astronaut House, Feltham, Middlesex, England

Copyright © The Hamlyn Publishing Group Limited 1970
Reprinted 1972 (twice), 1974, 1975, 1976 (twice), 1977, 1978, 1979
ISBN 0 600 00070 2

Phototypeset by Filmtype Services Limited, Scarborough, England
Colour separations by Schwitter Limited, Zurich
Printed in Spain by Mateu Cromo, Madrid

# CONTENTS

# INTRODUCTION

An aquarium, from the Latin, *aqua* – water, is defined by the Oxford Dictionary as, 'an artificial pool or tank for the keeping of live aquatic plants and animals. A place of public entertainment containing tanks'. We will, in this book, think of an aquarium as any container capable of holding water, fishes and/or plants and being inside a building. This does not include artificial or natural ponds outside. Places of public exhibition will be called Aquaria with a capital letter.

The keeping of aquaria has a long history. In 1596, Chang Ch'en-te wrote a book describing how he kept goldfish in tanks. Samuel Pepys wrote in his diary of 1665 (Lord's Day), 'My wife and I shown a fine rarity: of fishes kept in a glass of water, that will live for ever; and finely marked they are being foreign'. As early as 1853 a public Aquarium was built at the London Zoological Gardens and was the first public Aquarium in the world. In 1868, M. Simon the French Consul at Ningpo brought from China to Paris some Paradise-fishes *(Macropodus opercularis)* and gave them to Pierre Corbonnier. Later these fishes spawned in an aquarium.

In the Far East, young fishes are introduced into rice paddies as the rice is planted. Later fishes and rice are harvested together.

Triumphant young Amazon Indian with Pacu fish. The Pacu (*Colossoma* spp) is a rarely imported aquarium fish from northern South America. In the wild it feeds mainly on fruit.

Today several hundreds of species of tropical fishes are kept and bred in the home aquarium. Rare species are frequently imported and selective breeding and cross breeding have resulted in the improvement (though sometimes the worsening) of strains and the development of many varieties, to add colour to the home aquarium.

There is another aspect of tropical fishes which is perhaps not realized by most aquarists. These fishes provide food for many people in the tropics. They are hunted in various ways – by spear, poisons, fish traps and various types of net. Another increasing way of providing fishes for food is by fish farming and a number of species, particularly of the genus *Tilapia*, are being farmed. One way in which this is done is by putting young fishes in rice paddies when the rice is planted. Later, 5 inch fishes are harvested with the rice.

## Public Aquaria

Public Aquaria throughout the world have an obvious advantage over the ordinary aquarist in that they afford the space to keep many larger and more exotic specimens of tropical fishes. Cichlid fishes, for instance, are displayed to best effect in the vast tanks such as those at London Zoo, the Tower Aquarium, Blackpool and Belle Vue, Manchester. In addition to the aesthetic and entertainment value of these places, the fishes they keep are frequently of scientific interest.

In public Aquaria a great deal of thought has to be given to displaying the fishes to their best advantage. Many exhibit them in brightly lit tanks within a darkened room. Under such circumstances great detail can be observed both at the front and the back of the tanks and the eye is not distracted by surrounding decor. The fishes are usually divided into three main sections: cold freshwater fishes, seawater fishes and tropical freshwater fishes.

The services of all public Aquaria are large. There must, for instance, be reserve tanks for new arrivals to be quarantined and acclimatized, and also tanks for treating diseased fishes. Most Aquaria have a small breeding section to reproduce the more easily bred fishes. Many have complex systems of water

Excellent displays of tropical fishes can be seen at the Colombo Zoo Aquarium, Ceylon

Growing to 14 feet in length and 400 pounds in weight, the Arapaima *(Arapaima gigas)* is one of the world's largest freshwater fishes. It is occasionally seen in public Aquaria.

filtration and aeration. At Belle Vue Aquarium special tanks constructed of fibre glass are shaped to give an impression of no corners and a greater perspective is achieved. Aquaria in tropical countries, of course, are particularly fortunate in having easily available supplies of tropical fishes, and usually exhibit first-class displays.

The attractive Giant Gourami (*Colisa fasciata*) is popular in many public Aquaria. Gouramis are distinguished by their thread-like ventral fins, used as tactile organs.

# THE AQUARIUM

## Factors in selection

When purchasing an aquarium there are two main factors to be considered: size, which will be determined by the dimensions of the intended site, and weight, a factor which can be easily overlooked. The smaller 14 × 8 × 8 inch tank presents no problems but the larger tanks certainly do. A full 24 × 12 × 12 inch tank will weigh approximately one hundredweight and will, therefore, require adequate support. Any flat surface can quite easily be used to hold a fish tank, but it is sometimes preferable to use a stand, of which many kinds are available.

Most of the standard sized tanks can be purchased with a matching stand strong enough to bear the weight, but as the legs often have no feet, extra covering on floors may be required to spread the load. Metal stands are made in one, two or three tiers and if a unit of three 24 × 12 × 12 inch tanks is installed, the approximate total weight is around four hundredweight. It is therefore imperative that the unit is sited on a strong if not solid floor. It is always a good idea to purchase a two or three tier stand even if initially only one tank is purchased. The spare levels can be covered and used temporarily as storage spaces.

The weight of a full aquarium must be considered before purchase. As a guide, one cubic foot of water weighs sixty pounds.

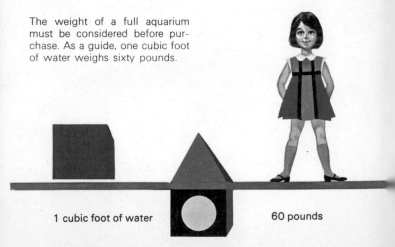

1 cubic foot of water          60 pounds

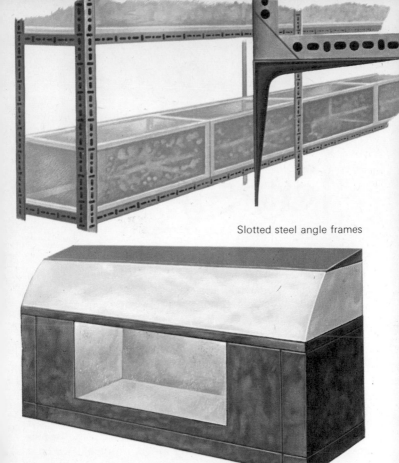

Slotted steel angle frames

A decorative stand incorporating a slotted steel angle frame can be readily assembled by the handyman

If the intending aquarist is a keen 'do-it-yourself' man he may wish to build a special unit using timber and hardboard etc., to fit exactly into a special space in a room. Care must be taken to make the main frame of sufficient thickness, remembering that if the cross members warp with the weight, a leaking tank may result. Another point to remember with this type of unit is the adequate provision for servicing both on

An attractive bow-fronted tank with a wrought iron stand

the facia and between the individual tanks. An ideal material for a special framework is slotted steel angle. This can be made up into virtually any size and shape and clad in a suitable material to finish it off. It is also easily dismantled for moving or decorating.

Although the waters of the earth vary considerably in temperature, an aquarium is usually classified as either tropical or cold. Normally this means that cold water aquaria adjust their temperature to their surroundings whereas the temperature of tropical aquaria is maintained artifically. Our native fishes have to withstand a temperature range from just above freezing point up to 60–65°F. Fishes from the tropics experience a much smaller yearly range, in some cases only one or two degrees, and the tropical aquarium is kept at 75°F with only minor variations all the year round. There are of course, fishes which live in intermediate temperature ranges and these can be adapted quite easily one way or the other provided extremes are not attempted.

The vast majority of private aquaria in this country are fresh water but with continual advance in techniques, marine aquaria are becoming more widespread. Many individual homes contain tropical fish tanks or aquaria simply for decorative purposes. The cheapness and availability of materials and equipment in recent years has greatly increased

Aquascapes, popular on the continent, display bog plants and fishes in shallow water

their popularity. Tanks adorn corners and recesses, fill holes in walls and can even form a living division within a large room.

It is also believed that the presence of tropical tanks can have a therapeutic effect. For this reason many public offices, doctors' and dentists' waiting rooms have them installed. Undoubtedly, the peace and colour of a well-kept tank does have a restful effect on the human mind.

The majestic *Pterois volitans*, one of the marine scorpion fishes

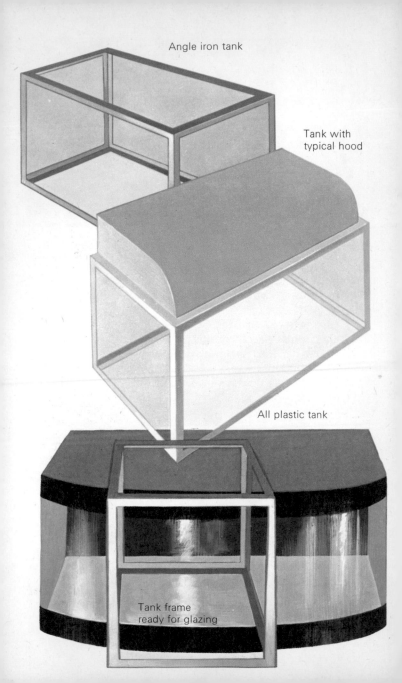

Angle iron tank

Tank with typical hood

All plastic tank

Tank frame ready for glazing

# Aquarium design

As rectangular tanks are most satisfactory their development in recent years has taken many forms. The frame is usually of angle iron to provide the necessary strength and rigidity, although the smaller tanks can safely use pressed steel. This type of tank, although the most commonly used, has the disadvantage of rusting easily around the top of the metal frame. To obviate this problem quite a number of alternative methods of construction have been employed.

Tanks moulded completely in glass are available from dealers in varying sizes, usually up to 15 × 10 × 10 inches. Care must be taken with these however, as one knock on a corner when moving usually means disaster. More recently the development of all-glass aquaria with the bottom, sides and ends of the glass sheets cemented together using silicon rubber cement has been very successful. These tanks can be made by the skilled handyman aquarist. Care must be taken to have the glass cut square and to carefully follow the instructions on the tube of silicon rubber cement.

For some years there has been on the market a tank made completely of plastic. It is not moulded from one piece but consists of flat sheets of clear and coloured perspex cemented together. Because of the flexible nature of the perspex these tanks cannot be constructed very large and in due course the front often becomes scratched.

More recently, an enterprising manufacturer has produced various sized tanks using fibre glass for the frame and base. Normal glass is used for the front, back and sides. These appear to have many advantages: the fibre glass is hard, can be produced in a variety of colours, and is non-corrosive. Another recent development, which has just been commercialized, is the sealing of angle iron frames by coating them with a layer of hard plastic before glazing. Some ingenious aquarists restricted by finance have made tank frames from wood, but this method is to be recommended only to the joiner with years of experience.

With so many types of tank to choose from cost is bound to have an effect on the final decision. The metal-framed tanks are usually cheapest in the range and the chromium-plated and fibre glass types more expensive.

The dimensions of the aquarium have an important bearing on the number and health of the fishes it contains. During life, like all animals, fishes take in oxygen ($O_2$) and give out carbon dioxide ($CO_2$). This process is called respiration. Dissolved oxygen is extracted from the water, and carbon dioxide, a waste product from the fish, is released in the water and finally escapes into the air. The amount of oxygen never becomes critical except under very unusual circumstances, but a high level of carbon dioxide can become poisonous to the fishes. This may happen when there are too many fishes in too small a tank, each fish producing its own quota of carbon dioxide. As this cannot escape quickly enough it accumulates in the water eventually killing the fishes.

A tank with a small surface area such as the typical goldfish bowl, through which less carbon dioxide can escape, is obviously potentially more harmful than one with the same volume of water but a large surface area, and shallow depth.

Plants in sunlight give off oxygen and absorb carbon dioxide so when the aquarium is lit this helps to reduce the amount of carbon dioxide present. This process, however, is reversed during the hours of darkness. Aeration by disturbing the surface of the water helps carbon dioxide to leave the water more easily, especially in a tank overcrowded with

The gill is the site of gaseous exchange in the fishes

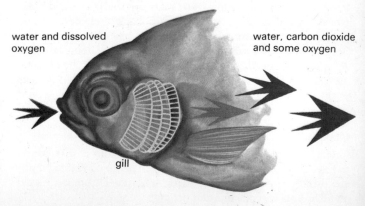

water and dissolved oxygen

water, carbon dioxide and some oxygen

gill

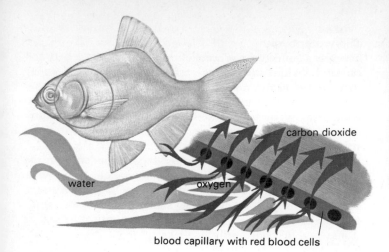

carbon dioxide

water

oxygen

blood capillary with red blood cells

In the gill, thin-walled capillaries are exposed to a flow of water from the mouth. Oxygen is absorbed from the water and carbon dioxide given up.

fishes. We have stressed the importance of carbon dioxide accumulation and not oxygen deficiency in all of these instances. Oxygen shortage occurs very rarely, only in those conditions of gross organic pollution of a tank, by over-feeding of dry foods or of *Daphnia*, which have subsequently died. The rotting of this food by millions of bacteria and protozoa make considerable biological demands on the oxygen supply.

A large surface area relative to depth is necessary for efficient gaseous exchange. Fishes are often seen gasping in goldfish bowls with small surface areas.

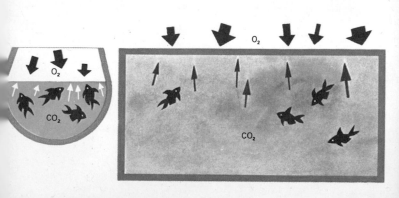

## Water
### The water cycle

There is a continuous process of exchange of water between the land, sea and atmosphere – the water cycle. Water vapour gets into the air by evaporation from the oceans, and to a lesser extent from lakes and rivers. Vegetation also gives off large amounts of water vapour to the atmosphere by transpiration from leaves. The supply is drawn from soil moisture by the root system of the plants.

Rainwater is formed when water vapour condenses in the atmosphere. This occurs when the water vapour in the air is cooled, either because it is forced to rise, or for other reasons. The total precipitation, including snow, frost, hail etc., finds its way back eventually by rivers and streams to the sea, or it may end up temporarily in a lake.

The water cycle in the earth-atmosphere system. Taps indicate sources of domestic water supply.

condensation of water vapour to clouds

evaporation

river

sea

No surface water is completely pure; soot, hydrocarbons and sulphur dioxide, especially in towns, chemicals in soil and rocks, and sewage effluent encountered on its course can be absorbed by the rainwater. The taps in the schematic representation of the water cycle below indicate the stages in the cycle at which domestic water supply is taken. The mineral constituents of river, reservoir and water from underground strata are seldom injurious to health. Such water is readily made available for human consumption by treatment to eliminate all disease-producing bacteria. Purification is accomplished by mechanical filtering out of bacteria followed by their destruction by other organisms and, finally, by chlorination.

The cycle is completed when the surface water is re-absorbed into the atmosphere and the process begins again.

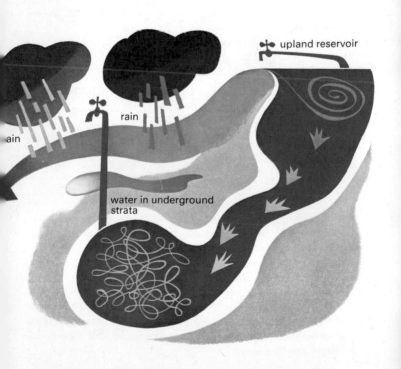

upland reservoir

rain

ain

water in underground strata

## The hardness of water

Pure rainwater, distilled water or demineralized water contain no other chemicals. Once rainwater passes through the ground however, it dissolves minerals contained therein.

One of the most common minerals is limestone (calcium carbonate, $CaCO_3$) and water containing excess amounts is said to be hard (temporary hardness). Other salts which make water hard are magnesium salts (permanent hardness). One of the common characteristics of hard water is that soaps lather very poorly. To the aquarist a knowledge of water types is important because fishes and plants thrive best where the degree of hardness is at the optimum level for the species concerned. The Neon Tetra *(Hyphessobrycon innesi)* for example, is at its best in soft water, whereas the Celebes Sailfin *(Telmatherina ladigesi)* prefers hard water. Hardness is therefore determined by the amount of $CaCO_3$ present in the water and this can be expressed in any of the three following ways:

(1) parts per million of $CaCO_3$ (ppm);
(2) grains of $CaCO_3$ per gallon (Clark degrees);
(3) parts of CaO per 100,000 (German degree DH).

Different books use different scales and it is useful to remember 1 Clark degree equals 14 ppm or 4/5 DH.

| Water description | ppm | °DH | °Clark |
|---|---|---|---|
| Soft | 0–50 | 0–2·8 | 0–3·5 |
| Medium | 50–150 | 2·8–8·4 | 3·5–10·5 |
| Hard | 150–300 | 8·4–16·8 | 10·5–21·0 |
| Very Hard | Over 300 | Over 16·8 | Over 21 |

Examples of fishes which thrive best in soft water include the Discus *(Symphysodon discus)* and *Pterophyllum* and *Aphyosemion* species, while the Celebes Sailfin *(Telmatherina ladigesi)*, *Bedotia geayi* and *Tanichthys albonubes* prefer water of medium hardness. The Platy *(Xiphophorus maculatus)* and the Sail-fin Molly *(Mollienesia latipinna)* on the other hand, require considerably hard water. It is difficult to be as specific about the requirements of plants. Like fishes some have wide tolerances, for example the cryptocorynes will flourish in virtually any fresh water.

## The *p*H value of water

The *p*H value of a solution is a number used to express its acidity or alkalinity and is an expression of the total number of hydrogen ions in the solution. Neutral water has a *p*H of 7, therefore water with a *p*H less than 7 has an acid reaction and water with a *p*H greater than 7 is alkaline. This scale is logarithmic so that water with a *p*H of 6 has a concentration of hydrogen ions ten times that of water of *p*H 7.

In nature the alkalinity of water is usually determined by its calcium carbonate and bicarbonate content. This of course, is also responsible for hardness. Although *p*H and hardness are separate factors in nature, hard water is nearly always alkaline. Acid water in nature is usually due to the presence of peat or decaying vegetation, conditions which tend to make water soft.

The acidity or alkalinity of water may be measured by using dyes which change colour according to changes in *p*H. For example, one drop of the B.D.H. Universal Indicator dye plus one drop of water is green at *p*H 7, blue at *p*H 8, orange at *p*H 6, etc. Such dyes are available as *p*H kits from pet shops.

Colours obtained from indicator dyes provide an estimate of *p*H

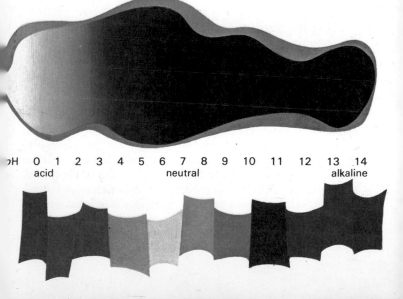

*p*H  0  1  2  3  4  5  6  7  8  9  10  11  12  13  14
　　acid　　　　　　　　neutral　　　　　　　　alkaline

Discoloration of the water results from disturbance of the peat layer *(left)*. Composts must be washed well before use in aquaria *(right)*.

## Aquarium equipment
### Composts

An aquarium compost is the gravel at the bottom of the tank in which plants can be grown. If a decorative tank is to be set up the compost used is usually one of the gravels commercially available from a pet shop. These comprise a mixed gravel, usually fairly light in colour and about $\frac{3}{16}$ inches in diameter. Coarser gravel makes rooting difficult and excess food and fish droppings tend to fall between the pieces and rot anaerobically – usually becoming smelly and black. If the gravel is too fine all the residue rests on the top of the gravel. Plant growth can be encouraged by a layer of peat or soil under the compost. It should be used with care however, for if a plant is uprooted for any reason, clouding of the water occurs. Planting sticks are useful for replanting (see page 142).

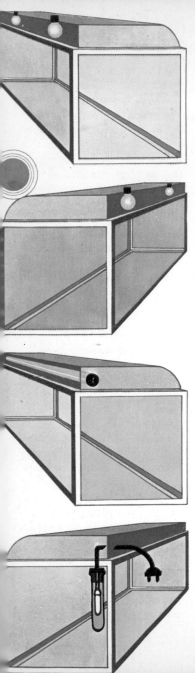

## Lighting

Lighting displays fishes to best advantage and helps plant growth. Most aquarists prefer to provide artificial lighting that they can regulate, rather than relying on daylight or ordinary room lighting. In any case, room lighting is useless for lighting an aquarium and a tank placed in strong sunlight will encourage algal growth, turning the water green.

One 25 watt light bulb, either 'clear' or 'pearl', per square foot of water is usually sufficient, if left on for about ten hours a day. Fluorescent tubes can be used in preference to ordinary light bulbs as these have a longer life. Tubes emitting light at the red end of the spectrum give better plant growth than white light tubes. A special tube for encouraging plant growth, 'Gro-lux', has been marketed in recent years.

Decorative lighting is popular with many aquarists. Underwater lighting, for instance, helps to heat the water as well as providing light.

Low wattage light bulbs provide sufficient light for most tanks (1). Direct sunlight causes algal blooms (2). Fluorescent tubes can be used (3), and units that provide heat as well as light (4).

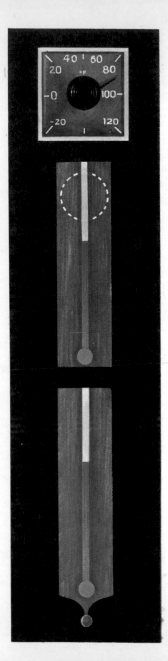

## Thermometers

As we have mentioned earlier, the temperature of aquarium water is very important, especially for tropical fishes. Too low a temperature makes fishes sluggish and more susceptible to disease but too high a temperature decreases the oxygen content of the water and the fishes will rise to the surface, gasping for air. With experience, the aquarist can usually tell if a large change of temperature has occurred, but it is always advisable to have a thermometer available. Ideal temperatures should be achieved before introducing fishes to the aquarium.

The most accurate type of thermometer uses mercury as the indicator and has the scale marked directly on the glass tube. These are rather difficult to obtain in the range required however, and one usually has to settle for something less efficient. The most common type available has the glass tube mounted on a scaled, clear plastic strip and held in position in the aquarium by a rubber sucker pad. Unfortunately, the colouring on the scale wears off, making it difficult to read. Spirit filled thermometers are cheaper but not so reliable.

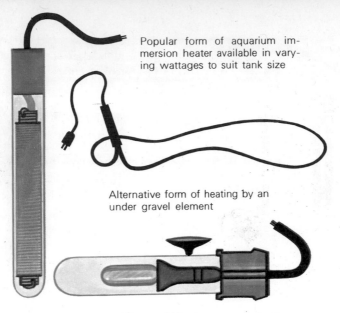

Popular form of aquarium immersion heater available in varying wattages to suit tank size

Alternative form of heating by an under gravel element

A lamp which also serves to heat the water

## Heaters

To maintain the required temperature in a tropical aquarium some form of heating is necessary. To the aquarist with only one or two tanks, electricity is the most efficient method. Gas and paraffin are far from odourless and the control equipment would be too bulky. Usually, the electric heater consists of an element wound round an insulated core and contained in a heat-resisting glass tube. A rubber cork with the electric cable held tightly through it acts as a watertight seal. Another method of heating by electricity is to place tubular space heaters (normally rated at 60 watts per foot) beneath the tank so that the heat rises to heat the complete unit. This method can be usefully employed if a faced-in unit has been constructed with adequate space between tanks, as the heat passing round the bottom tanks rises to help heat those on the upper layers. Care must be taken however, to either mount the heater away from the glass bottom or to place a baffle between the tanks, to avoid breaking the glass.

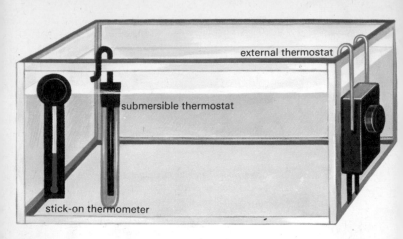

Tank above is fitted with two types of thermostat and a thermometer, and that opposite with three types of filter

## Thermostats

With the tropical aquarium it is necessary to control the temperature of the water within a range of 65–85°F, depending upon the species of fishes concerned. Aquarium thermostats are operated by contraction and expansion of a bimetallic strip at the end of which there are electric contacts. To reduce arcing and electrical interference a small magnet near these contacts provides a snap action.

There are two general types of thermostat. Firstly, there is the internal one which can be either fully or partly submerged in the water, the latter being clipped to the top frame of the tank, which means water levels cannot be allowed to fall very much. Secondly, the external thermostats are placed outside the tank fixed either by a metal clip or adhesive to the front glass. The manufacturer's instructions should be followed closely both in the wiring up and use of these thermostats. The temperature of any tank will always fluctuate a few degrees around the point set by the thermostat. This is a good thing as slightly varying temperatures are better for the fishes than an exactly constant one. In their natural environment all tropical fishes are subject to diurnal variations.

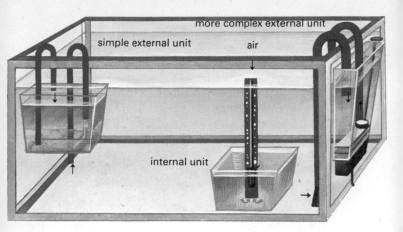

Filters are not essential items in aquaria, merely removing solid bodies from the water and not purifying it in any way

## Air pumps

Air pumps are used in the aquarium for two purposes: to force air into the tank and to work filtration systems. Aeration consists of forcing air by means of the pump through a small porous stone (diffuser). The stream of small bubbles formed agitates the surface of the tank allowing better exchange of carbon dioxide and oxygen. In a properly kept tank, not over-stocked with fishes, there is usually no need for aeration.

In filtration systems the pump pushes water through a filter which is either inside or outside the tank. The filter contains a filtration medium of charcoal, peat, nylon wool, plastic foam, etc., and particles passing through the medium are filtered off, keeping the water clear and freely circulating. Another type is the undergravel filter where the water is filtered through the aquarium compost. The common air pump is a small vibrator type which is very efficient but rather noisy in action. For the aquarist with more than four tanks the electrical induction motor type of pump is more satisfactory. This is quiet in operation and drives one or two pistons, usually by a rotary movement. Power filters are also very satisfactory but relatively more costly.

## Tank covers

Many species of tropical fishes enjoy a quick jump from their normal element. It is essential, therefore, to have some form of cover over the top of the aquarium. We have already mentioned that some form of artificial lighting will be required so this cover can serve to hold the light bulbs and also help to prevent evaporation. Normally these covers are made from aluminium, a metal which is easily worked, does not corrode too readily and also reflects the light fairly well. However in the special fibre glass tanks now produced the hoods are made of the same material. When made with a small lip on the bottom edges to fit neatly into the tank top, any evaporation condenses on the cooler metal and runs back into the tank. At this point we must emphasize that the wiring connected to the bulb holders must be well maintained and replaced when the insulation becomes brittle. If this is not done the risk of an electric shock is great. When tanks are placed in rows an individual tank top is not required and sheets of glass form ideal covers. This glass can either be laid directly on to the tank top or special clips can be used.

Tank tops resting on a top metal frame tend to cause rusting.

Aquarium covers also keep out dust and reduce heat loss and evaporation. A cover may take the form of a plain glass sheet with clips (*left*) or a metal hood (*right*) housing light bulbs.

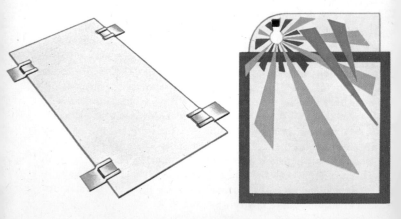

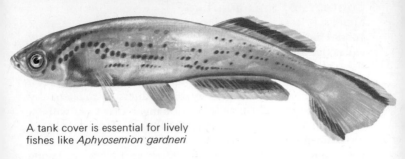

A tank cover is essential for lively fishes like *Aphyosemion gardneri*

To prevent this a grooved rubber strip can be fixed around the frame edge or, alternatively, the top frame can be treated with a cold galvanizing preparation. For the latter process the existing paint and rust must be removed (for instance by rubbing down with the sander of an electric drill), all the loose particles wiped off and the preparation applied with a brush. When dry two coats of paint are applied. This technique can be used on new and old frames and provides a very good protection from rust for many years.

'Galvafroid', a cold galvanizing process, protects tanks from rust

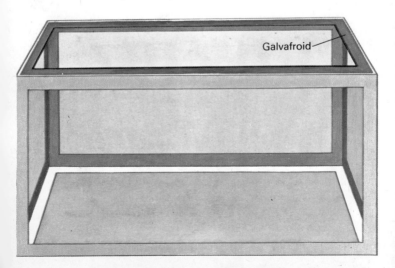

Galvafroid

## Contents of the aquarium
### Snails

While snails are not quite such an essential part of the healthy aquarium as is commonly believed, they will certainly consume some of the food left-overs, some algae and plants and decayed vegetation. They will not touch fish excreta however, and of course increase the waste products in the tank by adding their own. There is also a danger that they will eat living plants if other forms of food are lacking. Snails are introduced into the aquarium on plants, either as eggs or as very tiny newly hatched snails. Most reproduce by laying eggs in clusters contained in a jelly-like substance attached to firm objects such as rocks, glass or plants. When fresh plants are introduced to the aquarium it is nearly impossible to remove every egg without causing some damage to the plants. It is better to remove those which will come away easily and squash each tiny snail as it is noticed. If all are killed before maturity then the tank will remain snail free.

An aquarium plant with egg clusters, showing damage by snails

Red Ramshorn (1), *Bullinus* (2) and Malayan Snail (3)

One useful genus of snail, *Ampullaria*, is however, of use to the fish breeder in that the water in which it is kept breeds infusoria at a very fast rate. The snails are kept in a tank on their own and fed on lettuce or cabbage leaves. Care must be taken not to overfeed or the resulting odour is not very pleasant.

The most common variety of snail seen in tropical aquaria is the Red Ramshorn *(Planorbis corneus)*. Another snail in tropical aquaria, though not often seen because of its nocturnal habits, is the Malayan Snail *(Melania tuberculata)*. During the day, this snail spends its time burrowing into the gravel in search of food but at night it comes out, climbing all over the tank. It does not appear to eat living plants and as it reaches food which would otherwise decay in the gravel, it can be tolerated. It is live-bearing and therefore does not spoil the appearance of the tank with unsightly masses of eggs.

## Plants

Every aquarist should be able to grow healthy plants without too much effort. Anyone wanting to grow superlative plants or special plants will have to make special arrangements. Sometimes the requirements of the fishes and the plants clash. In the case of egg-laying tooth-carps, which do not like bright light, it is not possible to grow plants in tanks set up specially for breeding these fishes.

All plants have certain basic requirements. From the compost they get chemical salts such as calcium, phosphorus, nitrogen (as nitrates and nitrites) and very small quantities of other elements (trace elements). Fishes also help to provide nitrogenous substances in their droppings. In a tank which has been set up and undisturbed for many years plant growth tails off and we suspect this is due to the exhaustion of the gravel. We have known keen aquatic plant growers use 'Plantoids' under special plants in order to improve plant growth. Temperature is also important. Plants have a temperature at which they grow best and this is probably higher than the optimum temperature (72–75°F) for most fishes.

Some aquarium plants grow best as bog plants with their roots in water and their leaves in the air, though of course humidity has to be very high (see page 11). Seeds of some

A popular aquarium plant,
*Cryptocoryne beckettii*

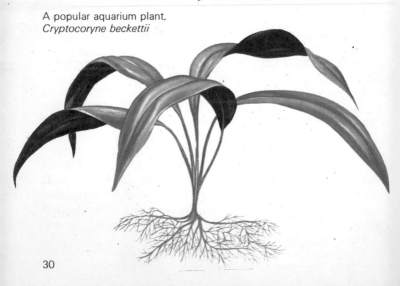

By photosynthesis, green plants manufacture sugars utilizing energy from the sun and carbon dioxide from the air

aquatic plants must be germinated as bog plants in this way. Light is tremendously important for aquarium plants – its intensity, how long it is kept on, and quality of the light all affect growth. Plants reared in a greenhouse with polythene double-glazing, for instance, may be retarded in growth because of the altered wavelength of light reaching them.

Other cryptocorynes grow well as bog plants

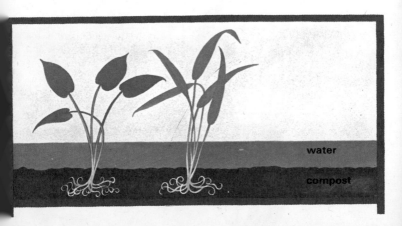

water

compost

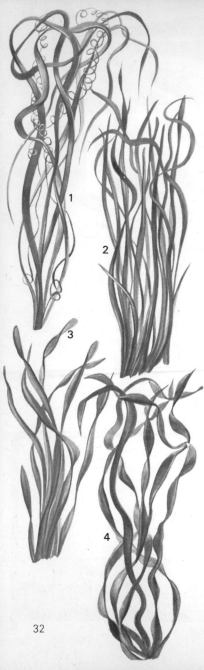

Plants of the genus *Vallisneria* are popular plants for aquaria. This genus originates mainly from tropical regions and although it is flower producing, seeds do not form in this country and it is propagated by runners.

1: *Vallisneria gigantea* is a large member of the genus with leaves up to 1 inch wide and 4 to 5 feet in length. It is more suitable for large, cold water aquaria as warm temperatures are not tolerated.

2. *Vallisneria spiralis* is the variety most commonly seen in tropical aquaria. The leaves normally grow up to 18 inches long and $\frac{1}{2}$ inch wide. If given plenty of light, the leaves will lengthen and spread over the surface but the runners will grow in profusion to provide the ideal background to the aquarium.

3. *Vallisneria spiralis tortifolia* is another very well-known variety commonly called 'twisted vallis'. The leaves grow to about 12 inches but are much more brittle than the straight *Vallisneria* and can be easily broken if treated roughly.

4. *Vallisneria spiralis 'contortionist'* is a variety recently introduced to the aquarium. The leaves are much more twisted than *tortifolia* and are longer, spreading over the surface like normal *spiralis*.

Plants of the genus *Sagittaria* are similar in appearance to those of *Vallisneria,* but are suitable for nearly all sizes of aquaria. They are propagated mainly by runners and some species grow naturally in bog conditions producing floating and aerial leaves.

5. *Sagittaria subulata* is the most common and popular plant of the genus. During spring and summer the leaves form narrow stems and spread into an oval, floating at the surface. This plant grows to a height of about 12 inches but there is a smaller variety growing to about 8 inches.

6. *Sagittaria latifolia* is a large member of the genus and therefore suitable only for the largest aquaria. It produces broad strong leaves up to 24 inches long. Under favourable conditions this plant will produce aerial leaves and occasionally flowers. It is suitable for both cold and tropical aquaria.

7. *Bacopa* produces bright green rounded leaves in pairs on ascending stems. When the plant has grown too tall it can be nipped off and replanted. *Bacopa caroliniana* is the best-known species.

8. There are three varieties of *Acorus* or 'Japanese Rush', two tall (one of which has yellow and green striped leaves) and one short. *Acorus* is a submerged bog plant which grows very slowly.

Without doubt, plants of the genus *Cryptocoryne* provide the aquarist with more colour and variety than any other. About a dozen species are known to the aquarist but there are about forty in the genus, originating mainly from the Malay Archipelago. Species vary in size from small plants only 1 or 2 inches high, to large ones up to 2 feet high. Leaves range in colour from pale green to deep red and their shape from slender and strap-like to broad and spade-like. However, the majority are really bog plants spending the rainy season totally submerged and gradually producing aerial leaves as the water evaporates. Because of this, many species are difficult to keep for any length of time, and those mentioned here will be hardy species generally obtainable.

Cryptocorynes have the advantage of growing very well in situations where the light is rather weak, but they are ornamental rather than useful plants. Their growth is slow and reproduction is by runners.

Nomenclature of the genus is often confused in the literature but the following classification is the one most commonly accepted.

1. *Cryptocoryne affinis* or *C. haerteliana*, is the most widely seen species with dark green upper surface and deep red underside to the leaves. Quite prolific, it grows to 12 inches. It thrives under subdued lighting.

2. *Cryptocoryne beckettii* is another fairly common variety, its leaves have a soft pale green upper surface and reddish brown underside. It grows to 10 inches.

3. *Cryptocoryne griffithi* is a temperamental species which takes time to settle down. It prefers soft water. The leaves are green on top and brown underneath.

4. There are two varieties of *Cryptocoryne nevillii*, one short and one tall, both having the same basic characteristics. The leaves are bright green on both sides.

5. *Cryptocoryne willissii* is a species which varies considerably. It sometimes grows by extending the crown and producing a type of rhizome as the leaves die off. The leaves are green on top and brown underneath.

6. *Cryptocoryne ciliata* is a large species, growing up to 18 inches with pale green leaves. It grows best as a bog plant when the leaves become heart-shaped and much shorter.

The genus *Echinodorus* includes some of the largest plants seen in tropical aquaria, and all originate from the Americas. Quite a few are naturally bog plants and if provided with plenty of light and space, will produce aerial leaves and flowers. If pollinated, seeds will ripen and many small plants can be propagated. When aerial flowers are not produced the flower stalk stays submerged and small plants develop at intervals along its length. All the species are green, varying from pale to dark, depending on the strength of light they receive. Leaf shape can be very variable especially with species producing aerial leaves.

1. *Echinodorus berteroi* (Cellophane plant) is a submerged plant, the older leaves of which are heart-shaped at the end of long stems. Aerial leaves and flowers are often produced.

2. Once established, the leaves of *Echinodorus cordifolius* remain the same shape whether aerial or submerged. When well fed, the leaves grow to 6 inches long and 4 inches wide and flower stalks are often produced in summer.

3. *Echinodorus martii* has long, strap-like leaves with wavy edges. Normally does not produce aerial leaves and the flower stalk, if kept submerged, produces small plants.

4. *Echinodorus paniculatus* (Amazon Swordplant) is the best known plant of this genus and has two distinct forms—one with narrow leaves and one with broad. The flower stalk normally stays submerged, producing plantlets.

5. The tiny *Echinodorus tenellus* (Pigmy Chain Swordplant) grows only 2 inches high and spreads by runners. It can easily become choked with blanket weed and care should be taken not to introduce the latter into the same tank.

6. *Echinodorus grisebachii* (Chain Swordplant) reproduces by runners along the surface of the compost and is easily cultivated. Careful handling of the delicate leaves is necessary.

7. *Echinodorus tunicatus* is a relatively recent introduction to aquarists with similar leaves to *E. cordifolius* but more pointed at the tip. The flower stalk tends to stay submerged and produce plantlets only.

*Aponogeton* species have a bulb or tuber from which roots and leaves develop. The plants go through a resting period during which the leaves die off but they reappear after a few months. Reproduction is from seeds produced on flower spikes above the water although some species produce side shoots from the rhizome. Tropical distribution is restricted to Africa, Asia and Australia and a number are peculiar to the island of Madagascar.

1. *Aponogeton ulvaceus* is a beautiful aquarium plant with latticed, semi-translucent green leaves. However, the leaves are easily torn and the plant tends to die back in winter. Becomes large under favourable conditions.

2. The leaves of *Aponogeton undulatus* are also translucent but have wavy edges. This plant can grow to heights of 6 to 8 inches depending on the light intensity reaching the tank. Imported as small bulbs or tubers.

3. *Aponogeton crispus* has pale green translucent leaves with crinkled margins. This species is fond of strong light and its narrow stems will adapt themselves to the depth of water in the aquarium. Propagation is by division of the tuber.

4. *Aponogeton fenestralis* (Madagascar Lace plant) is expensive and difficult to grow but a truly magnificent aquarium plant. The skeleton-like leaves consist of a mere lattice work of cross veins and do indeed resemble lace.

5. *Cabomba* is a plant that grows at a very fast rate and soon over-crowds the tank. Old stems should be cut back and new stems taken from the latest growth. There are two or three varieties with slightly varying leaves. This is one of the most beautiful aquarium plants but is not suitable for beginners.

6. *Hygrophila polysperma* has pale green lanceolate leaves and if kept pruned will produce an attractive bush. It will become straggly if left, however. Propagated easily from rooted cuttings.

7. *Ludwigia natans* is a common aquarium plant the leaves of which have a pale green surface with reddish-brown underneath. This plant has a tendency to grow up out of the water and really grows better as a bog plant.

8. *Myriophyllum* (Water Milfoil) is most suited to cold water but will survive in lower tropical temperatures. There are several species which resemble each other. Their fine, feathery foliage encourages spawning in breeding tanks.

9. *Nomaphila stricta* has large, bright green leaves. It is closely related to *Hygrophila* and also needs to be well pruned. It is a very attractive plant for most sizes of aquaria and grows well under most conditions.

1. *Azolla* is a very small green floating plant, sometimes known as 'fairy moss'. It forms a dense covering which varies in colour from brilliant green to a dark red in strong light. There are two or three varieties known to aquarists, all having the same characteristics.

2. There are two species of *Ceratopteris*, *C. cornuta* and *C. thalictroids*, known respectively as 'Floating' and 'Indian Fern'. Both plants reproduce by the formation of small plants on the edge of the leaves. In good light this is a very prolific plant.

3. *Lemna* is the Duckweed to be seen floating on most ponds. It normally has small, round leaves but one species *L. trisulca* has leaves shaped rather like ivy leaves. Some tropical fishes eat this weed and it is a good producer of shade in a tank where there is too much top light.

4. *Eichornia crassipes* (Water Hyacinth) has swollen leaf stems forming small buoyancy tanks to support the plant. This is a particularly showy plant for the large

aquarium, but needs strong daylight for good growth and therefore tends to die over winter. It produces an attractive short-lasting purple flower. Inset (4a) shows plant profile.

5. Commonly known as the Water Lettuce, *Pistia* has thick fleshy leaves and rather resembles a floating lettuce. In good daylight, runners are produced in profusion and the long thick roots offer perfect cover for young fry. This plant thrives in tanks without covers, exposed to daylight.

6. *Riccia*, sometimes known as Crystalwort, forms a floating mat just below the water surface. It sometimes becomes very thick however, and so periodically needs to be thinned. The pale green leaves offer perfect refuge for fry and in fact the plant is popular among breeders of livebearers. This plant is common in Australian waters.

7. The oval-shaped leaves of *Salvinia* are produced in pairs along the floating stems. It multiplies rapidly in strong light and quickly covers the aquarium surface. According to some authorities this plant has no roots—what appear to be roots are finely divided leaves.

8. *Najas* is a rather brittle floating plant which grows as well if anchored to the gravel. It needs regular pruning to prevent it from becoming too straggly. There are two or three species of this plant.

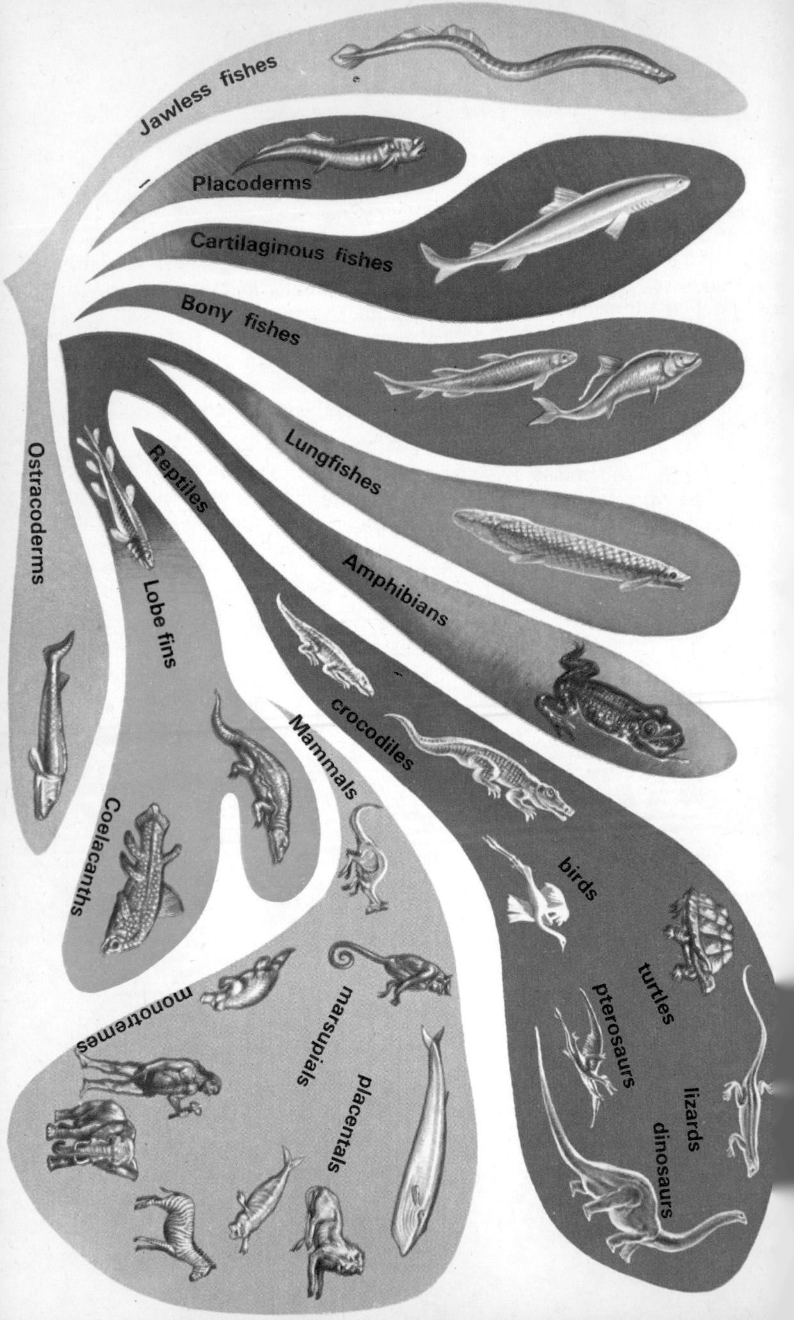

Jawless fishes

Placoderms

Cartilaginous fishes

Bony fishes

Lungfishes

Reptiles

Ostracoderms

Lobe fins

Amphibians

Coelacanths

crocodiles

Mammals

birds

monotremes

marsupials

placentals

turtles

pterosaurs

lizards

dinosaurs

# THE FISHES

## Evolution of the fishes

The evolution of fishes and modern animals is difficult to trace because the fossil record is incomplete. However, enough is known to suggest the general pattern of evolution and to reconstruct in some detail the history of groups in those areas where fossils abundantly occur. The chart opposite shows relationships among the major groups of vertebrates and those animals within a given colour probably developed from common ancestors.

Fossil evidence has demonstrated that the birds and mammals arose from the cold-blooded reptiles, the reptiles from the amphibians, the amphibians from some of the primitive fishes and the fishes themselves from even more primitive vertebrates, probably derived from invertebrate stock. The evidence also shows that the incredible number of diverse fish forms that exists today is but a fraction of the total number of fishes that have existed in the past, either in marine or freshwater environments. The existing forms have obviously been the most successful in the struggle for existence and may be considered, for the time being anyway, the topmost twigs of the fish family tree. The less successful forms, known to us as fossils, can be thought of as the lower branches, some of which are short, others longer and themselves branched. These will represent the earlier forms that perhaps flourished for a time but eventually failed to adapt to a change in their environment and so perished and became extinct.

The evolution of the early vertebrate larval forms to primitive fish-like forms is unrecorded in the fossil history of the fishes, probably because both forms were soft-bodied animals. By the time fish-like fossils were discovered, the jawless fishes, the cartilaginous fishes and the bony fishes were already differentiated from each other and are represented by a number of diverse and often specialized types.

Of these, the bony fishes have been the most successful and today are the most abundant, diverse and complex group of fishes. It has been estimated that 20,000 species exist, having adapted themselves to widely varying conditions in sea water, brackish estuarine environments and fresh water.

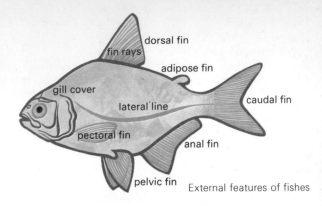

External features of fishes

## Physical structure of fishes

There are many modifications of the general external features shown above. The egg-laying tooth-carps (page 64) have a larger anal fin and large pectoral fins and some fishes, for example the Australian Rainbowfish *(Melanotaenia nigrans)* (page 114), have two dorsal fins. In the angelfishes the pelvic fins are considerably modified (page 110).

Fin rays are divided into hard rays (those with spines) and soft rays. The form and number of fin rays are characteristic of the species and expressed as a fin formula, e.g., D = dorsal fin, roman numerals indicate true hard rays, arabic numerals soft rays. Thus the dorsal fin formula of the Fire-mouth Cichlid *(Cichlasoma meeki)* is D.XV–XVI/9–10. Longitudinal and traverse scale counts are also characteristic of species and

Scales in purple are used in longitudinal and transverse scale counts

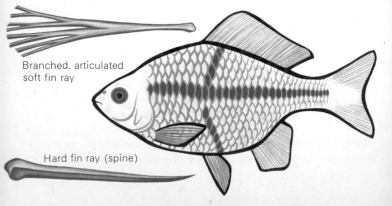

Branched, articulated soft fin ray

Hard fin ray (spine)

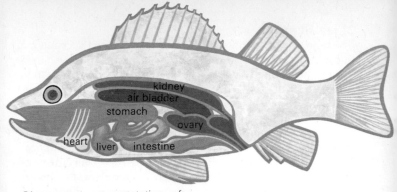

Diagrammatic representation of
internal organs of fishes

used in systematic identification.

The internal organs of bony fishes are much alike in general appearance. The function of the air bladder is not completely known but in several families, collectively called the Ostariophysi, it is connected with the auditory apparatus. The reproductive organs are paired and closely connected with the excretary system. Eggs are discharged from the ovary down the oviduct to the urogenital sinus and the exterior. The sperms are discharged from the testis, down the vas deferens which runs alongside the kidney and into the seminal vesicle which connects with the urogenital sinus. The skin consists of two layers, a thin epidermal layer and a thicker dermal layer which produces the scales and also the mucus which covers the body.

Humpy-back is a skeletal deformity that occasionally occurs in fishes

## Classification

Fishes, like most popular living creatures, have two names, a popular name and a scientific or Latin name. Popular names are easy to pronounce, are vaguely descriptive but can lead to a great deal of confusion. For·example, a Tiger Barb may be *Barbus tetrazona*, *Capoeta partipentazona* or *Barbodes hexazona*, depending upon which part of the world you live in. The scientific names on the other hand are fixed by international scientific agreement and are worldwide in application. This method consists of giving a fish a 'surname' (name of the genus to which it belongs) and a special name (species name) which is specific to that fish. For example, the popular Swordtail belongs to the genus *Xiphophorus* and is species *helleri*. The close relationship with the Platy is easily seen as the Platy is *Xiphophorus maculatus*. The specific name will sometimes describe a characteristic of the fish, e.g., *trilineata* (three lined) or may describe its origin, *senegalensis* (Senegal) or be named after its collector or describer. Occasionally a subspecies may exist and a third name is then added.

Fishes belong to the phylum Chordata, that is animals with backbones. Those in the super class Gnathostomata, are the more advanced fishes and of the fishes within this superclass the sharks and rays with cartilaginous skeletons form the class Selachii. All the fishes we will be considering are bony fishes

Common names often lead to confusion. *Gambusia afinis afinis* (1), *Gambusia afinis holbooki* (2) and *Heterandria formosa* (3) are all known as Mosquito fish

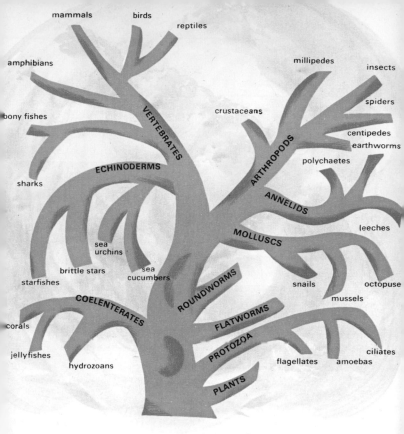

The animal kingdom can be represented as a tree on which the main branches represent *phyla*, and smaller branches *classes*

and are members of the class Osteichthyses.

These classes are further divided into orders and families and then into genera and species. It is of importance to the aquarist to know generally into which family a fish fits as genera in the same family tend to have similar habitats and breeding patterns. In the following section of the book, species from those families most popular among tropical freshwater aquarists are described and illustrated. The arrangement may differ from others found but classifications always vary slightly from authority to authority.

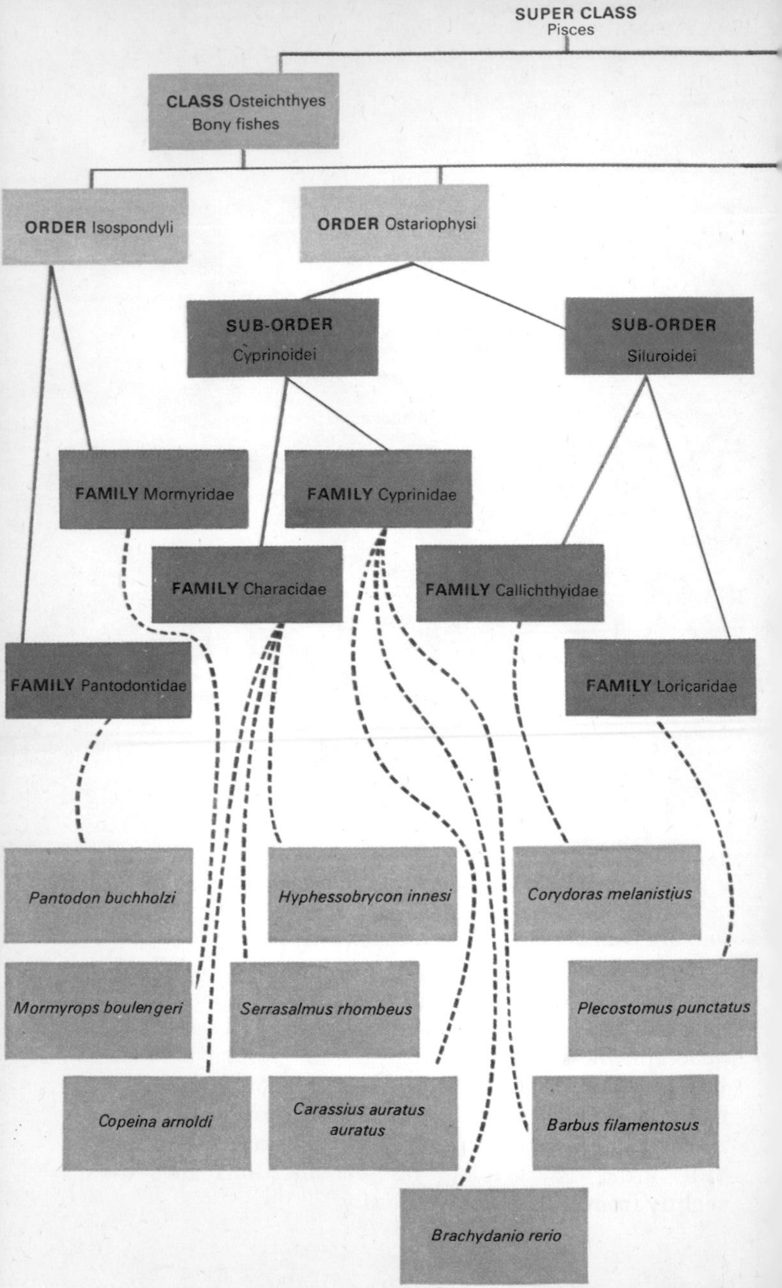

**SUPER CLASS** Pisces

**CLASS** Osteichthyes Bony fishes

**ORDER** Isospondyli

**ORDER** Ostariophysi

**SUB-ORDER** Cyprinoidei

**SUB-ORDER** Siluroidei

**FAMILY** Mormyridae

**FAMILY** Cyprinidae

**FAMILY** Characidae

**FAMILY** Callichthyidae

**FAMILY** Pantodontidae

**FAMILY** Loricaridae

*Pantodon buchholzi*

*Hyphessobrycon innesi*

*Corydoras melanistius*

*Mormyrops boulengeri*

*Serrasalmus rhombeus*

*Plecostomus punctatus*

*Copeina arnoldi*

*Carassius auratus auratus*

*Barbus filamentosus*

*Brachydanio rerio*

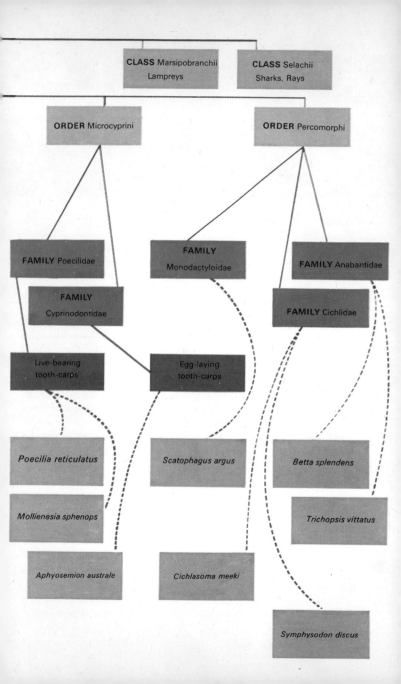

**CLASS** Marsipobranchii
Lampreys

**CLASS** Selachii
Sharks, Rays

**ORDER** Microcyprini

**ORDER** Percomorphi

**FAMILY** Poecilidae

**FAMILY**
Monodactyloidae

**FAMILY** Anabantidae

**FAMILY**
Cyprinodontidae

**FAMILY** Cichlidae

Live-bearing
tooth-carps

Egg-laying
tooth-carps

*Poecilia reticulatus*

*Scatophagus argus*

*Betta splendens*

*Mollienesia sphenops*

*Trichopsis vittatus*

*Aphyosemion australe*

*Cichlasoma meeki*

*Symphysodon discus*

Distribution of the live-bearing tooth-carps

## Family Poeciliidae (live-bearing tooth-carps)

From the map it can be seen that the live-bearing tooth-carps are restricted in nature to two parts of the world and in fact, as will be seen later, the majority comes from the Americas. Known technically as *ovoviviparous* fishes, they do not reproduce in the same way as mammals. That is to say, once the female has produced the egg, no further direct attachment to the mother takes place. The eggs are held within the female in a brood pouch and are fertilized there by the male. The eggs develop and later hatch but the young are not released until they have completely developed. By then, they are miniatures of their parents and within minutes of birth are capable of eating and swimming normally.

Nature has provided the male live-bearers with a special means of fertilizing the females. At puberty, the anal fin of the male undergoes a complete change, and bears no resemblance to that of the female. After the change the fin is called a *gonopodium* and is then used exclusively for the injection of sperms into the female.

Normally the gonopodium points backwards but when mating takes place, it is twisted forwards and sideways and the tip inserted in the female's vent. At this moment, the male ejects his sperms which travel along a groove in the gonopodium and enter the female to fertilize the eggs.

It takes about one month for the young to develop but this period can be varied by high or low temperatures. However,

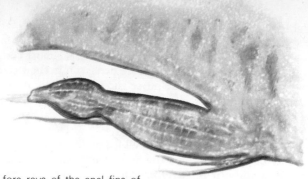

The fore-rays of the anal fins of males in this family are modified into a gonopodium

it does not follow that by increasing the water temperature the period of gestation will be shortened. The numbers produced in each brood can also vary quite appreciably; young females produce up to fifty offspring but the more mature they become the greater the numbers – up to 200 on occasions. Each female can produce four or five broods from the initial fertilization.

The professional breeder who wishes to maintain a good strain will remove all the males from the growing brood as soon as they are recognized. This prevents the females from being indiscriminately fertilized. Later the most suitable partnerships can be induced for the production of superior offspring.

It has been known for some time that some members of this family have been able to change their sex. This reversal seems to be encouraged by high temperature and usually occurs in spring and summer. The most quoted example is that of female swordtails developing a 'sword' and gonopodium before bearing young. These fishes have been used scientifically by the late Dr. Myron Gordon of New York in genetic studies and Dr. Alex Comfort of London in his research into the ageing processes.

In the Poeciliidae over forty species and sub-species are available to the aquarist, many colour varieties having been developed by cross and line breeding. If well fed and looked after they will live to five years according to size.

## Breeding live-bearers

Breeding live-bearers is not difficult. In fact, if there is a male and a female of the same species in a tank it is almost certain that they are breeding. The males are persistent in their court-ship giving the females little peace and within a few hours of placing them together the female will be fertilized. To be kind it is better to have two, if not more, females to each male to allow a little respite.

Most fishes, especially if not well fed on live foods, will eat their tiny offspring if given the opportunity and live-bearers are no exception. It is therefore imperative that some means of protecting the brood from their cannibalistic parents is provided. In the wild, as soon as they are born, the young instinctively head for the nearest cover. In the aquarium, if adequate cover is provided in the form of plants of various kinds most of the fry will survive. The ideal floating plants are *Riccia* and Indian Fern, and such plants as *Myriophyllum* afford cover at the bottom of the aquarium. This method is somewhat haphazard as no accurate count can be made and trapping needs to be adopted if all the brood is to be saved. Infusoria are not necessary as food except for fry of the smaller species and a few hours after birth fry of most species will eat dust-fine dried food. Food should be offered at least three or four times a day. The lengthening of the anal fin in the first few weeks distinguishes the males from the females.

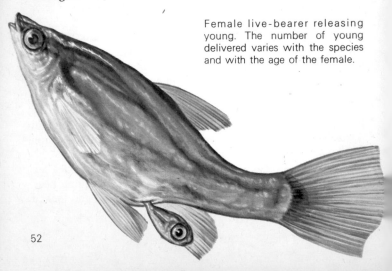

Female live-bearer releasing young. The number of young delivered varies with the species and with the age of the female.

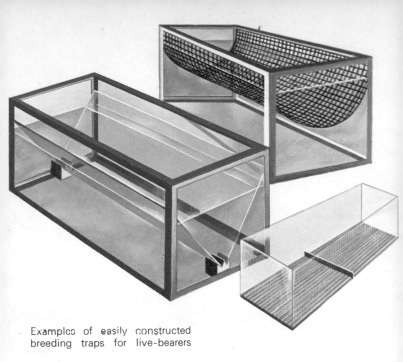

Examples of easily constructed breeding traps for live-bearers

When only one female is involved in breeding a commercially produced breeding trap can be used. This isolates the expectant mother in a small cage suspended within an aquarium. The fry when born escape to the main tank through narrow gaps in the bottom of the trap. Care must be exercised when transferring the female to the trap. If more than one female is to be used a much larger trap is required and the aquarist will have to make his own. With this method all males and females should live permanently in the trap. A large perspex box with glass rods in the base can be assembled but a much easier way is to use a plastic mesh. Use if possible a green coloured mesh with $\frac{3}{10}$ inch holes as this is the best. By cutting, bending and joining, large rigid 'nets' can be made and suspended in a large tank, the fry being able to escape in all directions. If large enough, up to a dozen pairs of adults can be accommodated in this way and virtually a continuous supply of offspring provided. Alternatively, a large trap can be assembled from V-shaped sheets of glass arranged as shown above.

Examples of wild types of Guppies (1, 2) from which the other more elaborate varieties shown have been bred. The Green Lace Guppy (3) for example, has a beautiful lace pattern on the body and the Scarf-tail Guppy (4) has a tail often. much longer than the body of the fish.

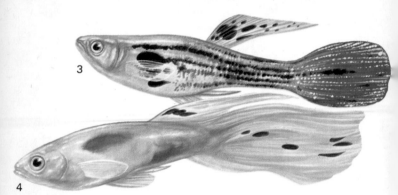

## The Guppy (*Poecilia reticulatus*)

This is the most common of all tropical fishes seen in aquaria, because of its low cost and hardiness. Many people start off with a few Guppies before purchasing other more expensive types, and in spite of inevitable errors made at first they usually survive, eventually to breed.

A native of some of the islands of the Caribbean and the bordering countries of South America, the wild fish is quite plain in comparison with its aquarium-bred relatives. From these insignificant fishes have come the most beautiful and varied hybrids and many aquarists have given up all other

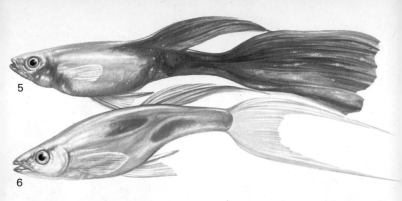

Because of its magnificent tail the Veil-tail Guppy (5) is possibly the most popular of all hybrids at present available. Females of the Golden Double Sword Guppy (6) exhibit an attractive golden colour. Other Guppy strains can be distinguished by their dorsal and tail fins (7).

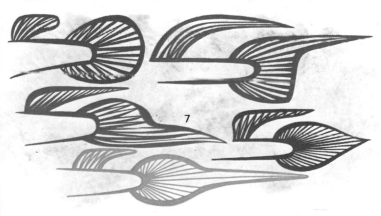

fishes to specialize in Guppies alone, becoming internationally well known for their special strains. Until recently, the females have changed very little, but now, by selective breeding, colour is appearing in the tail. The males have shown amazing development, and the illustrations show some of the strains that have become 'fixed'.

The mixed strain from the dealers stock tank can be bought quite cheaply, but if the aquarist wishes to purchase a new or special strain, he must expect to pay a considerably higher price for the time and patience of the breeder.

Black Sail-fin Molly
(*Poecilia latipinna*)

## Mollies (*Poecilia* spp)

Although popular live-bearers, members of this particular genus are not so easy to keep as those of the genera *Lebistes* and *Xiphophorus*. All the members of the genus come from South and Central America and the water in which they live is hard and alkaline and the normal temperature is around 80°F, higher than that recommended for the community tank. This combination produces an appreciable growth of algae, which forms a large part of the diet of these fishes.

To maintain the fishes in good condition, these requirements need to be met in the aquarium and it is advisable therefore to provide them with a special tank to themselves. As these fishes also frequent brackish water in nature, a small quantity of salt, say one teaspoonful to the gallon, can be added to the aquarium. The mouth of the molly is turned upwards so they are well equipped to take dried food and if fairly strong lighting is used algae will be provided naturally. Dried foods with a vegetable content should be used if possible.

It is possible to breed these fishes in outdoor ponds during the summer months, for the fishes will tolerate a temperature range of 60–90°F.

*Poecilia sphenops* is the short-finned member of the genus and the originator of the Black Molly. Widespread in natural

distribution it is more hardy than *latipinna* and will adapt itself
to the community aquarium fairly well. Unfortunately, because
of continual line breeding the average length attained by this
fish is only about 2 inches, although really good fishes will
reach 3½ inches. These are usually bred by the enthusiast by
introducing new blood regularly into his strain. The species
varies considerably in coloration but in general the colouring
of the female is more uniform than that of the male.

The Sail-fin Molly (*Poecilia latipinna*) is by far the more
attractive molly but is more demanding in its requirements.
The male of the species develops a very large sail-like dorsal
fin, reaching to an inch above the fish. The normal form has a
metallic blue background colour with dots of yellow, red and
green. By crossing with the Black Molly and then line breeding
the progeny, a molly with a black sail fin has been produced –
a magnificent fish, but very rare.

A further species, the Giant Sail-fin Molly (*Poecilia
velifera*), is similar to the Sail-fin Molly except that as the name
suggests, it grows slightly larger, growing to a length of 5 to 6
inches under good conditions. Aquarium specimens rarely
reach a length of more than 4 inches however.

Giant Sail-fin Molly
(*Poecilia velifera*)

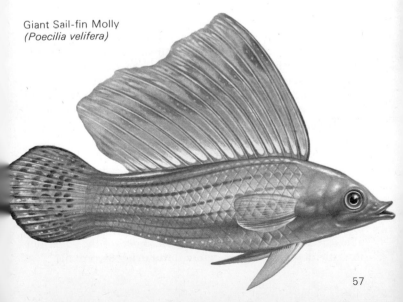

## Swordtails and platies (*Xiphophorus* spp)

The Swordtail *(Xiphophorus helleri)* is another fish, which by selective breeding has produced a wide variety of colours but without changing the basic body and fin shape. However, the native fish of this species, known as the Green Swordtail, is very attractive and can still be seen in many tanks. Unfortunately, by continuously breeding from the same strains, the fishes have been reduced in size and it is a rare specimen that measures up to the wild fish of 5 inches. Distributed from Southern Mexico to Guatemala the wild males and females are approximately the same size if the male's sword is disregarded. Males are slimmer in outline than females.

Very often this fish is selected by the beginner because of its colour but it is not always a wise choice. Because Swordtails grow fairly large the other inmates of the tank tend to move away when one approaches. Very often the males chase the other fishes and also appropriate much of the available food, aggravating the situation by their increasing size. It is advisable, therefore, to allow the smaller members of the aquarium to settle down and grow before introducing Swordtails.

The normal variety Green Swordtail (1) is still popular with many aquarists. The Red-eyed Swordtail (2) as its name suggests has red eyes. The Red Wagtail Swordtail (3) displays jet black finnage. It is an attractive fish and very popular among aquarists. 'Simpson' Swordtail (4) is a mutation from America, named after its breeder. By further interbreeding the flowing dorsal fin has been passed on to all the known types. The patterns on the Berlin Swordtail (5) look haphazard but in fact the general outlines have been fixed. By further line breeding an all-black fish has been produced.

To obtain the best results when keeping Swordtails, large tanks should be used to allow space for the fishes to move and grow. As with the mollies some algae should be included in their diet, although with Swordtails it is not quite so important. It must be remembered that if more than one type of Swordtail, or for that matter two different members of this genus are in the same aquarium, cross breeding will take place. If the types are to remain pure then a separate aquarium for each is essential.

The related Platy *(Xiphophorus maculatus)* is shorter, has a more solid appearance and, most important, has no aggressive tendencies. The males, except for the gonopodium, are like the females but slightly smaller and slimmer and do not develop the typical sword of the Swordtail. The Platy was once mistakenly thought to be a member of the genus *Platypoecilus* from which the popular name was derived. Many hybrids have been produced.

The Platy is a hardy fish, makes few demands and is undoubtedly a most suitable live-bearer for the beginner. With a little experience and one or two spare tanks the aquarist can try his hand at producing his own hydrids. As with other live-bearers, Platies prefer hard, alkaline water with a temperature between 75–80°F. If the aquarium is well lit, sufficient algae for their needs will develop naturally.

Another species of this genus often seen in the Variegated Platy *(Xiphophorus variatus)*. Hybridization has taken place

The sequence of crosses involved in producing the platy variety Golden Wagtail. The first cross is between a gold and a wild grey platy.

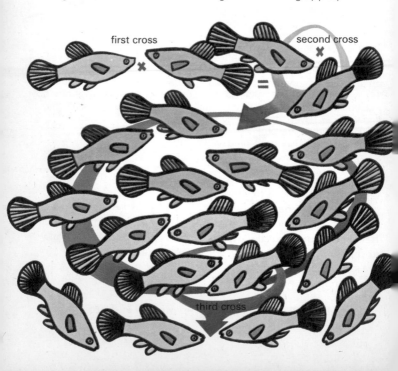

Two male Variegated Platies *(Xiphophorus variatus)* chasing a female, with the variety Red Platy *(top left).*

and also cross breeding between this and other members of the genus. The main characteristic is that the male and the female do not always have the same colour patterns. The female generally has an overall golden colour with very little of the colour contrasts displayed by the male.

The Platies are much more reliable breeders. They can be left with their young with reasonable safety, provided the parents are well fed and the tank is well planted.

## Other live-bearers

The Pike Top Minnow or Pike Live-bearer *(Belonesox belizanus)* must be given its own tank and fed only on live foods, preferably small fishes. When adult at 6 to 8 inches it can eat most small fishes in a tropical aquarium, and in fact is the largest species of live-bearer.

Pike Top Minnow (1); Mosquito Fish (2); Dwarf Top Minnow (3);
One-sided Live-bearer (4)

The Mosquito Fish *(Gambusia affinis)* although only a small fish is not popular because of its tendency of fin-nipping. It is used extensively in natural mosquito control in the tropics as each fish can destroy its own weight in mosquito larvae every day. It is usually plain grey but in a sub-species *G. holbrooki*, the males are nearly all black.

The Dwarf Top Minnow *(Heterandria formosa)* is the smallest of the live-bearers, the males reaching a maximum of only one inch, the females a little larger. They are best kept in a tank of their own when they will multiply rapidly if well fed.

The One-sided Live-bearer *(Jenynsia lineata)* is not often seen in the aquarium, the older males tending to be aggressive. The males are very interesting scientifically because of restricted movement in the gonopodium – in some it is movable to the left, in others to the right. 'Right-handed' males can only mate with 'left-handed' females and vice versa.

The Hump-back Limia *(Limia nigrofasciata)* is the most attractive member of its genus. The males develop the hump at maturity. Broods are small in number, with a longer gestation period than usual. A trap is necessary for breeding as the females tend to eat the young. The dorsal fin in the male becomes enlarged and fan-like with age.

The Blindfish *(Amblyopsis spelaeus)* originates from southern North America and is rarely seen in Britain. This very interesting fish has many sensory vibratory receptors on the head and body.

The Half-beak *(Dermgenys pusillus)* is one of the few live-bearers from the 'old world'. It is not easy to keep, requiring such foods as *Daphnia* and mosquito larvae. A small quantity of salt in the aquarium is beneficial for breeding and a trap is necessary. The fishes tend to float just below the surface.

*Anableps anableps* is rarely seen in the aquarium but is of interest in that its eyes are mounted in elevated sockets enabling it to see above the surface. The sexes are 'right- and left-handed' and only opposites can mate as in *Jenynsia*.

Hump-back Limia (5); Blindfish (6); Half-beak (7); *Anableps* (8)

Distribution of the egg-laying tooth-carps

## Family Cyprinodontidae (egg-laying tooth-carps)

Members of this family are very closely related to the live-bearing tooth-carps. They are small fishes with interesting breeding habits, and have relatively large mouths well filled with teeth enabling them to eat other species smaller than themselves. They need soft, acid water, temperatures between 68–73°F, prefer live food and dislike bright light. They are excellent jumpers so tanks must have tightly fitting lids. For breeding purposes they can be classified as *egg-hangers*, which lay their eggs on the roots of floating plants, or *egg-buriers*, which bury their eggs in mud at the bottom of ponds.

Examples from the two groups of egg-layers

**Egg hangers**
Asphanius
Panchax
Oryzias
most *Aphyosemion* spp
Chriopeops goodei
Jordanella florididae
Fundulus
Rivulus
Cubanichthys cubensis
Valencia hispanica
Aplocheilus
Aplocheilichthys
Micropanchax
Epiplatys
Pachypanchax

**Egg buriers**
Roloffia occidentalis
Aphyosemion sjoestedti
Cynolebias
Rachovia brevis
Cynopoecilus
Pterolebias
Nothobranchius

## Breeding egg-hangers

To breed these fishes very soft water (under 50 ppm $CaCO_3$) is necessary, and rainwater or a mixture of demineralized water and tap water can be used. The next operation is to dissolve four handfuls of natural peat in rainwater, bring it to the boil, allow to cool, and squeeze dry. This peat should be added to the rainwater in the breeding tank, where it will settle on the bottom in a few days. The boiling treatment adjusts the $pH$ of the peat to between 5·5 and 6·5.

A breeding mop for the tank can be made from a cork and nylon wool and is much more suitable than floating plants as it can be sterilized. The mop should be situated in the darkest corner of the tank for the fishes do not favour light.

When preparations are complete one healthy male should be placed with three females in the tank. Very soon he will drive the females around and eggs are laid two or three at a time, perhaps on several occasions each day, onto the mop. In one week 250 eggs may be laid by good fishes. The male is so virile that if he is given only one female he will kill her.

At the end of the week the mop can be removed to a jam-jar with water from the tank and the eggs incubated at 68–73°F. If a new mop is put in the tank the adults will continue to spawn. The eggs will take fourteen to twenty-four days to hatch but developing embryos are easily seen at the end of one week. If the mop is not removed from the tank after one week, well developed fishes may eat the newly hatched fry.

Breeding tank with peat layer suitable for egg-hangers

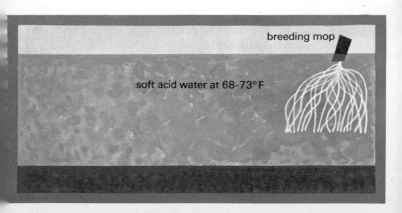

breeding mop

soft acid water at 68-73°F

# A selection of egg-hangers available to the aquarist

*Rivulus cylindraceus* comes from Cuba and Florida and grows to about $2\frac{1}{2}$ inches long. It is a good leaper, and needs a close fitting cover on the tank. It is said to leave the water to rest on top of floating leaves.

*Aplocheilus lineatus* grows to 4 inches. It has a large mouth and tends to eat any fish smaller than itself. One male needs more than one female when spawning. It lives in the wild in drainage ditches, pools, ponds and streams.

The Firemouth Panchax *(Epiplatys dagetti)* comes from West Africa. It swims just under the water surface waiting for food. A typical egg-hanger, it is fairly robust and lives well in the community tank. It can be a prolific spawner.

*Pachypanchax playfairi* originates from East Africa and is a large and tough member of the family. Its large mouth renders it unsuitable for the community tank. Like all the egg-laying tooth-carps, it is a valuable fish in the wild for malaria control as it consumes large amounts of mosquito larvae.

*Aphyosemion australe* is certainly a very beautiful member of this genus which does well if given the correct conditions. It originates from West Africa. Females of species in this family are drab compared with the males and tend to resemble each other. To avoid confusion therefore it is important not to mix females if more than one species are kept.

*Aphyosemion gardneri* has become an extremely popular fish in recent years and is very easy to breed if given the right conditions. The colours in the dorsal and caudal fins are particularly variable. This fish forms hybrids with other aphyosemions.

*Aphyosemion bivittatum* is another very pretty fish and spawns in the same way as other egg-hangers. This fish is slow to mature and is six months old before breeding begins.

*Aphyosemion cognatum* may lay as many as fifty very sticky eggs in a day all over the mop. In an extensive study of these fishes, the B.A.S.S. (see page 153) found thirty per cent of all eggs laid were infertile and that the fertile eggs hatched in fifteen days at $72°$F.

*Rivulus cylindraceus* (1); *Aplocheilus lineatus* (2); Firemouth Panchax (3); *Pachypanchax playfairi* (4); *Aphyosemion australe* (5); *A. calliurum* (6); *A. bivittatum* (7); *A. cognatum* (8)

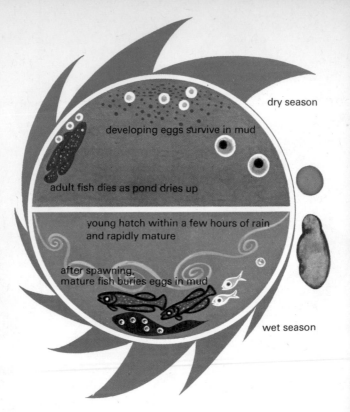

Within the diagram:

dry season

developing eggs survive in mud

adult fish dies as pond dries up

young hatch within a few hours of rain and rapidly mature

after spawning, mature fish buries eggs in mud

wet season

Diagrammatic life cycle of the egg-buriers

### Egg-buriers

These fishes have a fascinating life cycle in the wild as the parents die of asphyxia when ponds dry up during the dry season. The Dwarf Argentine Pearlfish *(Cynolebias nigripinnis)* provides an excellent example of the breeding habits of the egg-buriers.

The tank should be set up as for egg-hangers but without the mop. One male is usually placed with three females. If two adult males are placed with females very fierce fighting takes place. The male will court the females, dashing from one to the other and eventually one of the females will begin to spawn and they will dive together into the peat and com-

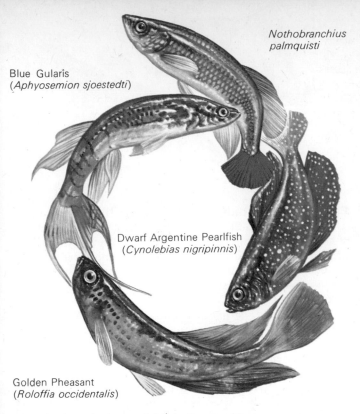

Blue Gularis
(*Aphyosemion sjoestedti*)

*Nothobranchius palmquisti*

Dwarf Argentine Pearlfish
(*Cynolebias nigripinnis*)

Golden Pheasant
(*Roloffia occidentalis*)

Example of egg-buriers available to the aquarist

pletely disappear. After about twenty seconds the male will emerge followed ten seconds later by the female, leaving an egg buried in the peat. The spawning process is repeated but after ten days the females become thin and are best removed and reconditioned for a week before being put back with the male.

The peat should be filtered through a nylon net which holds back the mould containing the eggs. It is advisable to put this in a plastic box and to leave it for a few days, until it has become moderately dry. A lid should be put on the box, which is then incubated at 68–70°F for sixteen weeks. Then, if soft acid water is added the fry hatch within twelve hours.

Tiger Barb

Minnow

## Family Cyprinidae (carps or carp-like fishes)

The carps or carp-like fishes consist of about 1,500 species some of which are important food fishes. Many are small but some of the larger barbs, *Barbus tor* for example, can grow up to 100 inches in length. Goldfishes, many tropical species and well-known coarse fishes such as Roach, Tench and carp, belong to this family.

The Minnow *(Phoxinus phoxinus)* is a cold water European cyprinid and one of the popular 'tiddlers' caught by small boys. Aquaria for minnows should have a gravel bottom, fresh water and aeration. They take all live foods and a shoal will spawn on the bottom in water less than 6 inches deep.

The Goldfish *(Carassius auratus)* is the domesticated variety of the Asian sub-species known in China for 1,000 years. Goldfishes eat both vegetable and meaty foods and will spawn in large tanks and ponds. The grotesque shapes produced in

Goldfish

Comet Goldfish

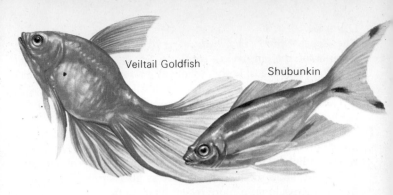

Veiltail Goldfish

Shubunkin

goldfishes have been exploited by the Chinese and Japanese and line breeding has given rise to various fancy varieties. The Comet, for example, is very similar to the typical cultivated form of the Goldfish except for its very long caudal fin. The Veiltail has greatly elongated fins and is golden in colour. Throwbacks to the wild type sometimes occur in spawning. The Telescope Veiltail is similar but has protruding eyes. The Shubunkin is a very common variegated form of the Goldfish, with colours of deep blue, red and white, black and golden. First-class specimens are expensive and the standards for showing internationally determined. The Egg-fish has a stocky egg-shaped body with fins only moderately developed. There is no dorsal fin and the caudal fin is short and often double. The Celestial has a similar body form but has prominent globular eyes, upwardly directed. The Lionhead is an Egg-fish in which the head is expanded with warty outgrowths.

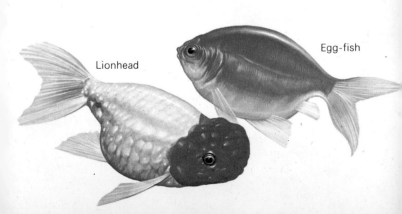

Lionhead

Egg-fish

## Danios

The Zebra Danio *(Brachydanio rerio)* is probably the most popular of the egg-laying tropicals. Because it is hardy and easy to breed its cost is always low. It is an active fish and likes to have plenty of room to swim, as do all the danios.

The Pearl Danio *(B. albolineatus)* and the Spotted Danio *(B. nigrofasciatus)* are similar in shape to the Zebra Danio. The former has a silver body with an iridescent, mother-of-pearl effect giving differing colours depending on the angle of reflected light. The latter has stripes down the lateral line and numerous spots below. Their size is also similar, reaching 2 to 2½ inches long. A more recent introduction is the Leopard Danio *(B. frankei)* which has a body pattern very much like our native trout. The Giant Danio *(Danio malabaricus)* grows to 4 inches and although large, is a peaceful fish.

Breeding all species can be accomplished easily by placing a pair of fishes in shallow water with a layer of previously sterilized pebbles or marbles in the bottom.

Zebra Danio (1); Pearl Danio (2); Spotted Danio (3); Giant Danio (4)

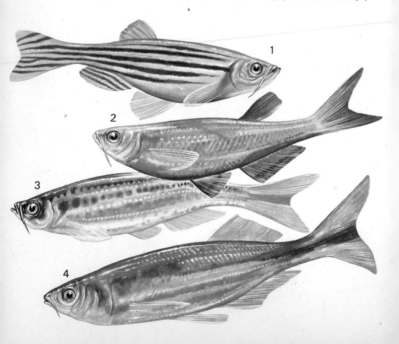

## White Cloud Mountain Minnows

Found in the streams of the White Cloud Mountain in China, there are two distinct fishes grouped under the same common name. The fish usually seen is *Tanichthys albonubes,* the other is *Aphyocypris pooni,* the only difference in appearance between the two being a yellow edging to the fins of the latter.

These are peaceful little fishes, ideal for the beginner as they are undemanding in their requirements. These fishes are not true tropicals in nature and therefore high temperatures are not appreciated, 70–75°F being most suitable. Spawning is easy. If two or three pairs are placed in a well-planted tank they will spawn and the fry will not be eaten if the parents are well fed. The young are even more attractive than the adult fishes. The lateral line develops into a brilliant green stripe when the fry are about $\frac{1}{3}$ inch long, far outshining the Neon Tetra at this stage. Unfortunately, as the fish grows this line of colour loses much of its brilliance, fading into a creamy stripe but the fins turn to yellow and red.

*Aphyocypris pooni* (5); *Tanichthys albonubes* (6); fry (7)

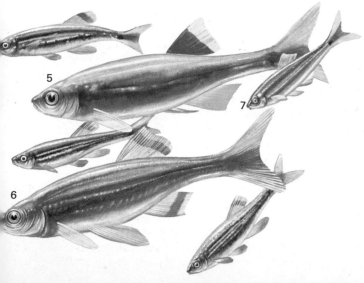

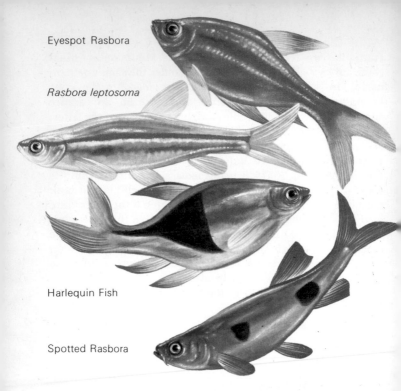

Eyespot Rasbora

*Rasbora leptosoma*

Harlequin Fish

Spotted Rasbora

A selection of rasboras suitable for inclusion in the community aquarium. Most are shoaling species and probably 'community breeders'.

## Rasboras

All natives of South East Asia, members of the genus *Rasbora* are difficult to breed and as a result most fishes are imported from that area, mainly Singapore. The Harlequin Fish *(Rasbora heteromorpha)* is so common in the wild that it can be caught and flown to Britain to sell at a price cheaper than if it had been bred artificially. This species is, however, the only one regularly seen, others are shipped in every now and then but their prices are usually above average. All species prefer soft, acid water at temperatures between 75–80°F and a well-planted aquarium providing areas of light and shade. They are peaceful fishes and if possible should be purchased in a group as they like to shoal. They eat nearly anything, but prefer live foods such as *Daphnia* and micro-worms.

The Spotted or Pygmy Rasbora *(Rasbora maculata)* measures only one inch in length at maturity, whereas the Scissors-tail *(Rasbora trilineata)* grows to 4 inches.

## Barbs

Though a number of American authorities split the genus *Barbus* into *Barbodes, Capoeta* and *Puntius,* in this book they are all classified as *Barbus.*

Most barbs are active, even boisterous, and do not like over-crowding, preferring a well-aerated, well-planted tank. The majority have large scales producing changes in pattern under differing lighting conditions. They all breed readily in the aquarium.

Most common is the Tiger Barb *(Barbus tetrazona)* one of the most colourful and active of the barbs. It has an unfortunate tendency to nip the fins of other fishes but this is not so important when other barbs are involved. Males are distinguishable by their red 'snouts' and brighter colours. Some varieties of barbs are described over page.

A pair of Tiger Barbs showing sex differences

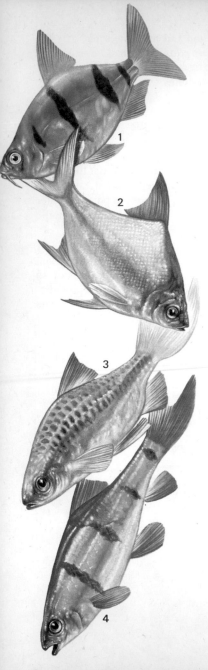

*Barbus hexona* although a very pretty barb, is not often seen as it is difficult to breed and does not travel well. It grows to 2½ inches, is quiet and spends most of its time among the plants.

The Tinfoil Barb *(Barbus schwanenfeldi)* is a really beautiful fish but outside the scope of the average aquarist as it grows to at least 8 inches. It needs a predominantly vegetable diet or it will begin to eat the aquarium plants.

The Checkered Barb *(Barbus oligolepis)* is easy to keep and breed and because of its size it does well in small tanks. It is a very attractive fish and grows to 2 inches in length. The males are most colourful at breeding time.

Females of the Half-banded Barb *(Barbus semifasciolatus)* grow larger than the males, reaching 3 inches in length. The males have an intermittent black line along their sides but the females only the odd dot. The variety Golden Barb is probably related to *Barbus sachsi*. This is a fish without any striking beauty and yet is very popular with many aquarists.

*Barbus hexona* (1); Tinfoil Barb (2); Checkered Barb (3); Half-banded Barb (4)

The males of the Cherry Barb *(Barbus titteya)* develop a deep red colour when spawning and are not as intense at other times. When breeding this species, shallow water and plenty of plants help prevent the parents eating the eggs. This is a quiet fish, ideal for the beginner and growing to about 2 inches.

The male Rosy Barb *(Barbus conchonius)* also exhibits brilliant mating colours. With black fins and deep red body turning to green on the back he puts his mate to shame. Her colours are similar but far less brilliant. This is one of the hardiest of the barbs.

The Nigger Barb or Black Ruby *(Barbus nigrofasciatus)* grows to about 2½ inches and is also brilliant when spawning. The male's colours are from deep red at the nose to jet black at the tail.

The Two-spot Barb *(Barbus ticto)* is not a well-coloured fish but is nevertheless popular. It grows to about 2½ inches and its large scales shine with reflected light. The dorsal fin of the male is trimmed with red, and this becomes intense during breeding.

Cherry Barb (5); Rosy Barb (6); Nigger Barb (7); Two-spot (8)

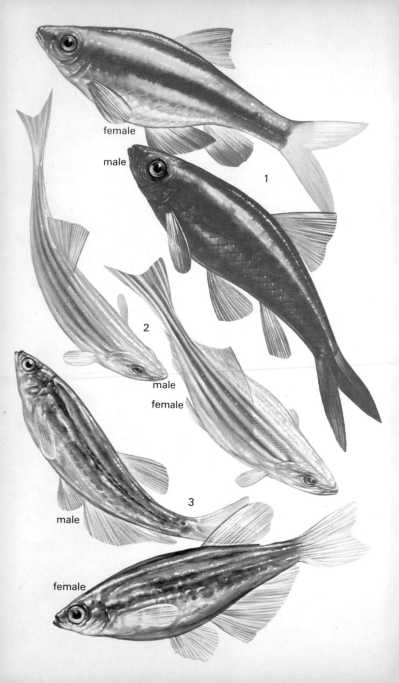

female

male

1

2

male

female

male

3

female

## Breeding danios and barbs

Generally speaking, breeding danios and barbs is easy and can be accomplished by most aquarists with a little experience and patience. Rasboras are difficult and should be left to the expert.

Danios and barbs spawn in a similar manner, although they lay different types of egg and an individual set-up is required for each. When a male and a female are placed together the male will start courting his mate by swimming around her with his fins spread to the full. This usually impresses the female and she will respond by following him around. They will start to nudge one another until they both become very excited. Then, swimming side by side they tremble, the female releasing eggs, the male milt. The eggs immediately absorb water and sperm and are fertilized. This process continues until the female has released all her eggs and at this point it is best to remove the fishes. Through their exertions they will have developed a hearty appetite and they will quickly make a meal of the eggs they have just produced if allowed to.

The eggs take from one to four days to hatch, according to species. Hatching, the fry look like small slivers of glass hanging around the tank. If a magnifying glass is used it will be seen that these fry still have a large yolk sac and it takes a further day or two of development before this disappears and the fishes are swimming freely. At this stage, food is required in the form of infusoria (minute organisms) for two or three days followed by brine shrimp until the fry can take small *Cyclops* and *Daphnia*. The practice of rearing fishes on nothing but fine, dry food is not to be recommended.

It is surprising how often aquarists' attempts to breed a particular species of fish have been unsuccessful because of the amazing fact that the fishes involved were not even a pair. An amateur is recommended to purchase at least half a dozen healthy young fishes. As they develop a close watch will reveal the sex differences and a true pair can be obtained.

Pairs of Cherry Barbs (*Barbus titteya*) (1), Zebra Danios (*Brachydanio rerio*) (2) and Leopard Danios (*Brachydanio frankei*) (3) showing sex differences

When an attempt at breeding is to be made it is best to segregate the sexes for a period of a week or two and to feed with as rich and varied a diet as possible to bring the fishes to the peak of condition. During this period, the spawning tank can be prepared. As both danios and barbs will readily eat their own spawn, some sort of protection is necessary. The eggs of the danios do not adhere to material objects, as do some. A breeding trap made of plastic mesh of the type suggested for the live-bearers is therefore recommended. This should be fairly large to allow plenty of swimming space. A simpler method, however, is to wash and clean a 16 × 8 × 8 inch tank and cover the bottom with a layer of marbles or pebbles previously sterilized by boiling. Water should then be added to provide 2 to 3 inches of swimming depth. Fresh water should be used but the pH and hardness are of no real importance. The temperature should be around 80°F. A pair of fishes placed in this tank one evening usually spawn the next morning and should be removed once the spawning is completed.

Arrangement of breeding tank for barbs

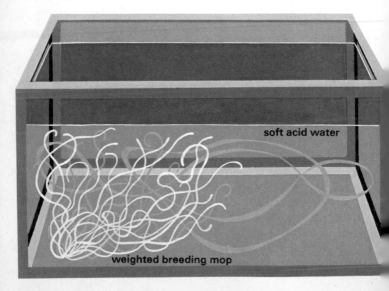

soft acid water

weighted breeding mop

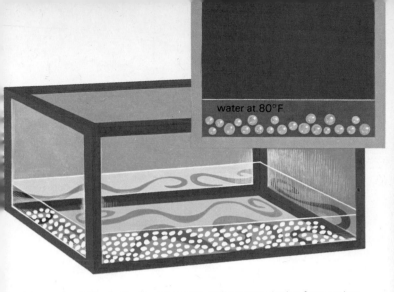

A layer of pebbles in the breeding tank will prevent danios from eating their eggs

After spawning the fishes will be tired and the female especially will be much slimmer. The eggs when laid will drop to the bottom and fall into the crevices where the fishes cannot find them. Water of the same temperature should now be added to almost fill the tank so that the fry have plenty of room when they hatch.

The eggs of the barbs are slightly adhesive and therefore need modified provisions. The tank size also needs to be larger – at least 18 × 10 × 10 inches. This should be filled with fairly soft (100 ppm) and slightly acid (pH 6·6–6·8) water. At one end, large clumps of sterilized coconut fibre or nylon mops should be placed so that the fishes will be attracted to that end to spawn. The whole tank can be loosely filled with coconut fibre just as effectively. The fishes spawn in and over this medium and can of course eat any eggs visible if not removed once spawning has finished.

When the fry of both types are free swimming they will need a lot of food, though care must be taken not to overfeed or pollution may occur. Mild aeration will help to prevent the danger of pollution.

Gourami (*Osphronemus goramy*)

Exposed gill chamber of a labyrinth fish to show the labyrinth organ

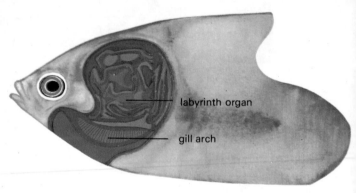

labyrinth organ

gill arch

## Family Anabantidae (labyrinth fishes)

There are over thirty-eight species of labyrinth fishes known to aquarists, sizes ranging from $1\frac{1}{2}$ inches to 2 feet. The distinctive feature of members of this family is the possession of a special respiratory organ which allows the fishes to breath atmospheric air.

The labyrinth organ consists of concentrically arranged bony plates, with a vascular membrane, enclosed in an enlarged gill cavity. The fish comes to the surface and takes in a mouthful of air, which is then forced into the labyrinth where gaseous exchange occurs. This labyrinth organ allows the Anabantidae to live in oxygen-poor water and to survive longer in polluted tanks in which other fishes will die. However, anabantids are not really suitable for the community tank as they tend to bully other fishes.

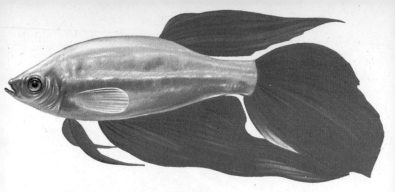

Varieties Cambodia (*above*) and
Blue fighting fishes (*below*)

The Siamese Fighting Fish *(Betta splendens)* from South East
Asia is a beautiful and easily kept fish and the first egg-layer
a beginner should attempt to breed. In the wild it lives in
ponds and irrigation ditches. The male is extremely aggressive
towards other males and in Thailand fights are staged between
male fighting fishes very much as cock fighting used to be in
England. This fish requires no special $p$H or hardness of
water but prefers a shallow tank containing some plants.
The tank should be in a well-lighted position and have a
temperature of 72–82°F. Adult males cannot be kept together
but one male and a few females do well together in a community tank. The fins of the female are always small and un-
imposing whereas those of the male are well developed and
magnificently flowing.

Adult male (*left*) and female (*right*) *Betta splendens*

## Breeding Siamese Fighting Fishes

A male and female must first be selected and conditioned separately, being given plenty of live foods. It is recommended that the bottom of the breeding tank is painted black on the outside and that it contains no gravel. The male should be put into the tank in the evening and later a jam-jar containing the female can be introduced. Next morning, when the female is gently turned out, the male will begin to court her.

During courtship the male chases the female and swims alongside her extending his gill covers and fins. He then begins to blow a bubble-nest among the floating plants [1]. The bubbles adhere and a nest up to 4 inches in diameter and half an inch above the surface may be built.

Breeding tank with floating weed suitable for 'fighters'

When the nest is completed the male drives the female up under it, she turns over on her side and he wraps himself around her [2]. She releases a few eggs and these are fertilized as both fishes drift slowly downwards. The male picks up the eggs and blows them into the nest. The embrace is then repeated until the female is empty of eggs. At this stage the male becomes aggressive towards the female and if she is not removed he will almost certainly kill her.

The male tends to the eggs until the fry hatch [3]. Some fall out and spiral away to the bottom but are picked up and blown back by the male. After about five days the fry are free swimming and the male should then be removed. The fry should be fed with infusoria or fine egg yolk for a few days and then given freshly hatched brine shrimp. Later, micro worm, screened *Daphnia* and chopped Whiteworm can be given.

Not every attempt to spawn 'fighters' may be successful; young fishes may eat their eggs, or the male may not look after them after hatching. The fishes should be reconditioned and put together about a month later.

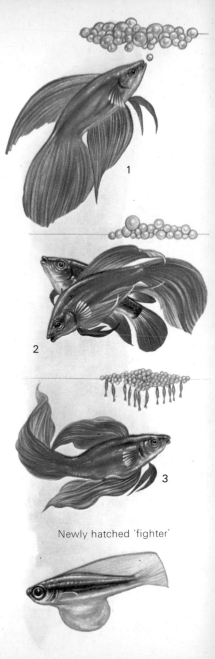

Newly hatched 'fighter'

## Popular labyrinth fishes

The Climbing Perch *(Anabas testudineus)* is not a perch and does not really climb. It can, however, use its tail to 'walk' several hundred yards on land from one stretch of water to another, propped up on its pectoral fins and gill covers. During these excursions the fish uses its labyrinth organ to breathe moist air.

Unlike most labyrinth fishes the male of the Javan Mouth-breeding Fighting Fish *(Betta brederi)* incubates the eggs in its mouth. They hatch after two days and are released after five days by which time they are free swimming.

The Honey Gourami *(Colisa chunae)* is a small fish just over $1\frac{1}{4}$ inches in length. The male builds a nest which may cover a large area of the tank. Spawning is similar to the Siamese Fighting Fish but the eggs float and at 80°F hatch in twenty-four hours.

The dorsal and caudal fins in both sexes of the Comb-tail Paradise-fish *(Belontia signata)* have extensions or

Climbing Perch (1); Javan Mouth-breeding Fighting Fish (2); Honey Gourami (3); Comb-tail Paradise-fish (4)

Paradise-fish (5a); mutant albino form (5b)

filaments, giving the appearance of the teeth of a comb. This fish, which originates from Ceylon, can be rather boisterous. The nest is a very flimsy affair and may consist of a few well dispersed bubbles only among the floating plants. The eggs float and hatch in two days. Parents should be removed or alternatively the eggs can be spooned off into a separate container, immediately after spawning.

The Paradise-fish *(Macropodus opercularis)* comes from the Far East and was probably the first tropical aquarium fish. It is a very hardy fish and can be kept outdoors in garden pools in summer in the south of England. It grows to 4 inches in length and the male is more highly coloured and has larger fins than the female. These fishes can be kept at 60–70°F, though raising the temperature to 78°F stimulates spawning. The spawning procedure is very similar to that of the Siamese Fighting Fish. Occasional specimens can be pugnacious, especially towards smaller fishes and must be introduced into the community aquarium with care.

A mutant albino form sometimes occurs and is very popular among many aquarists.

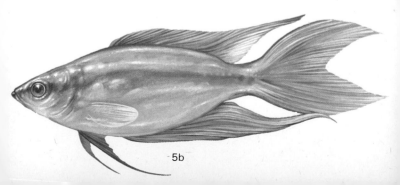

5b

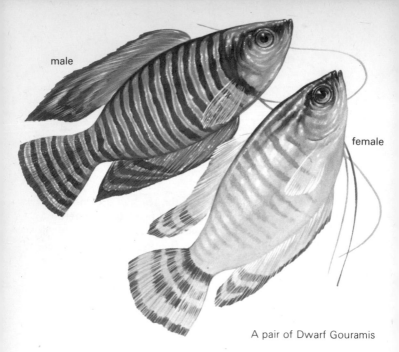

male

female

A pair of Dwarf Gouramis

The Dwarf Gourami *(Colisa lalia)* is a very colourful member of the labyrinth family and grows up to 2 inches long. A peaceful, hardy fish, but very shy, it tends to hide among the plants and only come out for food. For breeding purposes it is important to choose males with unbroken, and as near perfectly matching transverse bars as possible. About eight young fishes are usually reared together in a well-planted tank. After a while the males develop their breeding colours and the females get very plump. The selected pair should be placed in an 18 × 10 × 10 inch tank with a water depth of 4 inches, and the top covered with various floating plants. No gravel is needed. The temperature should be slowly raised to between 78–82°F and before long the male will build a bubble nest, reinforced with small pieces of plant, and spawning will occur. It is advisable to remove the female immediately but the male can be left until the eggs hatch. About 200 eggs are laid in a good spawning and they hatch within thirty-six to forty-eight hours. They are very small and should be fed infusoria. At about two weeks they are ready to eat brine shrimp and micro-worm. If fifty fry reach maturity the aquarist has done very well.

The Kissing Gourami *(Helostoma temmincki)* from South East Asia is yellowish silver all over. These fishes have the habit of 'kissing' each other with everted lips.

The Chocolate Gourami *(Sphaerichthys osphromenoides)* is a difficult fish to keep in the aquarium and there are conflicting reports on its requirements. The Chocolate Gourami is reported as a mouth-brooder.

The Pearl or Mosaic Gourami *(Trichogaster leeri)* originates from South East Asia. Immature fishes are difficult to sex but when mature, the female has a more rounded dorsal fin and is plump. The male builds a large bubble nest.

The very common Three-spot Gourami *(Trichogaster trichopterus trichopterus)* can grow up to 6 inches in length. These fishes are easy to spawn and they breed in the usual anabantid way.

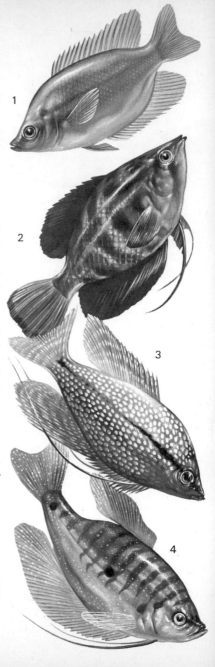

Kissing Gourami (1); Chocolate Gourami (2); Pearl Gourami (3); Three-spot Gourami (4)

Distribution of the characins

## Family Characidae (characins)

Members of this family form one of the largest freshwater fish families in the world. They are represented to the aquarist in about one hundred species and there is considerable variation among them. As will be seen from the map the world distribution of this family is restricted to the African and American continents but the percentage of aquarium fishes from Africa is very low. The Amazon basin of South America with its maze of waterways and streams is continually providing new species as scientists probe further inland. As yet, vast areas are still unexplored and will undoubtedly provide numerous specimens suitable for the aquarium.

All characins possess either teeth or an adipose fin and very often both. The adipose is a small, nearly transparent fin situated on the back of the fish just in front of the caudal and can be called the 'trade mark' of the characins. Members of this family like live foods in variety but will also take dry foods quite readily.

Characins come in all shapes and sizes and therefore suit all tastes. Specimens vary in length from an inch to over 1 foot and from long and slender to flat and compressed. Some species like a fair proportion of vegetable matter in their diet and if insufficiently provided, will play havoc with plants. The majority of the smaller species are peaceful fishes and suitable for the community aquarium but the larger fishes are more aggressive.

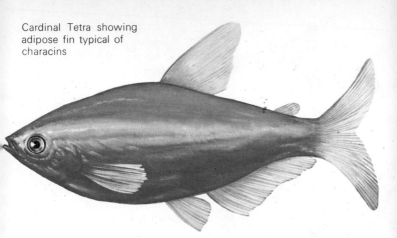

Cardinal Tetra showing adipose fin typical of characins

Some species are easily bred, others are extremely difficult. Some of the popular species fall into this latter class and as a result their prices remain high. Quite a number of the species from South America are known as tetras and one of the most common is the Neon Tetra *(Hyphessobrycon innesi)*. It is doubtful if any other fish has been described in print more frequently and most aquarists dream of one day spawning some of these beautiful fishes. Professional breeders have mastered the art as the fishes can be purchased very reasonably and are always in good supply. Unfortunately, the Neon Tetra is susceptible to a disease 'plistophora' or 'neon disease', which appears as a whitish patch on the body beneath the dorsal fin. No cure is known and as it is suspected of being contagious, infected fishes should be killed immediately.

In 1956 in America, a fish with even brighter colours than the Neon Tetra made its first appearance and was named *Hyphessobrycon cardinalis*. Later this was changed to *Cheirodon axelrodi* but its popular name of the Cardinal Tetra still remains. Both commercial breeders and experienced aquarists now successfully breed this fish. Shaded tanks, with soft acid water, are essential to the well-being of all the characins. Other characins of the genus *Hyphessobrycon* are described overpage. This genus is popular with many aquarists, the fishes being colourful, hardy and quite undemanding. They are somewhat difficult to breed however.

Lemon Tetra

Rosy Tetra

Bleeding Heart Tetra

*Hyphessobrycon serpae*

The Lemon Tetra *(Hyphessobrycon pulchripinnis)* is an old favourite although not brilliantly coloured. It grows to 2 inches and can be spawned fairly easily. Plants should be provided in the breeding tank however, to reduce the chances of the eggs being eaten.

The Rosy or Black Flag Tetra *(Hyphessobrycon rosaceus)* is one of the most beautiful characins. The males have longer dorsal and anal fins than the females. These fishes prefer soft, acid water and look their best in subdued light in a shoal. They are somewhat difficult to spawn.

The Bleeding Heart Tetra *(Hyphessobrycon rubrostigma)* is similar to *H. rosaceus* but larger and not so colourful. It grows to 3 inches in length but is not too easy to keep and relatively difficult to spawn.

*Hyphessobrycon · serpae* is very similar to *H. callistus* but smaller and a brighter red in colour. The shoulder marking is a small dot. Like all the red coloured characins, these fishes look their best in a shoal. This is one of the more beautiful small aquarium fishes but not often seen. It is a restful, quiet fish.

The Bentos Tetra *(Hyphessobrycon bentosi)* is not very common in Britain but is becoming more popular. It grows to about $1\frac{1}{2}$ inches long and is closely related to *H. callistus.*

Bentos Tetra

The body colour of *Hyphessobrycon callistus* is pale red and the fins are black. The fish has a black vertical bar on the shoulder and measures about $1\frac{1}{2}$ inches in length. This fish is very similar to *H. serpae* with which it is sometimes confused.

*Hyphessobrycon callistus*

The Red or Flame Tetra *(Hyphessobrycon flammeus)* rarely lives up to its name. Possibly as a result of continuous line breeding, the red colour has paled to a rose tint in most fishes. However, this tetra is very undemanding and breeding is easy, even in hard water. For small fishes, these are long-lived, and survive for three to four years. The recommended temperature range for the species is 70–80°F.

Red Tetra

The Black Neon *(Hyphessobrycon herbertaxelrodi)* was introduced to aquarists in the early 1960s and in soft, acid water is really quite attractive. Males are about $1\frac{1}{4}$ inches long and females about $1\frac{3}{4}$ inches, which makes sexing easy.

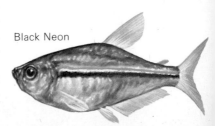

Black Neon

*Hemigrammus ocellifer*

The characins of the genus *Hemigrammus* are also South American, from the Amazon basin. *Hemigrammus ocellifer*, commonly known as either the Beacon Fish or the Head-and-tail-Light Fish, is not a brilliant fish but when settled in an aquarium it produces bright splashes of colour. The spot in the base of the caudal fin glows golden and the top half of the eye is golden red. The tips of all the fins have a splash of white. Sex can often be determined before the fishes are adult as the males have a faint white bar crossing the anal fin. At maturity, the females are larger and plumper than the males.

The more recent introduction of *Hemigrammus ocellifer ocellifer*, with the extra black and gold spots on the flanks, has replaced the original fishes somewhat and as they are easily bred they are always available. Where possible, at least half a dozen should be purchased as they are more attractive in a shoal. This fish seems to be more susceptible than most to

*Hemigrammus ocellifer ocellifer*

White Spot disease so extra care should be taken when purchasing.

The Glowlight Tetra *(Hemigrammus erythrozonus)* has caused a lot of confusion over its name. Sometimes it is known as *Hemigrammus gracilis* and it has even been placed in the genus *Hyphessobrycon*.

This fish is often overlooked in the dealer's brightly lit tanks because the body is often pale and the line along the body faded to a dull orange. Tetras do not like strong light as a rule and the Glowlight is no exception. However, if kept in a well-planted and moderately lighted aquarium the body becomes a soft, translucent brown and the line turns bright

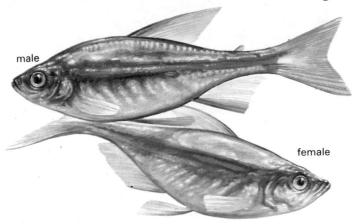

An adult pair of Glowlight Tetras

red. A splash of red appears in the base of both the dorsal and anal fins and all the fins have white tips.

Not many years ago, this fish was expensive as it was not easy to breed, but it is now one of the cheapest and can be spawned quite easily if the right conditions are provided. Glowlights grow to about only 1¾ inches in length and do not like the company of larger fishes. As with the Beacon Fish, at least half a dozen should be purchased and introduced to a tank containing other small fishes, preferably characins. Adult males are slightly smaller and slimmer than adult females, as shown in the illustration above.

male

A pair of Spraying Characins (*top* and *bottom*)

The Spraying Characin *(Copeina arnoldi)* has one unusual claim to fame – its method of reproduction. To protect its eggs from underwater predators, this fish lays them on some object, usually overhanging vegetation, about an inch above the surface. The pair of spawning fishes move towards the surface and then together leap clear, clinging long enough to the spawning ground to lay and fertilize a few eggs. They then drop back into the water, repeating the exercise until they have laid up to one hundred. At this point the male takes over, driving the female away. The spawning site in the wild may be a large leaf or plant stem, but in a half filled aquarium, a long piece of slate protruding above the water a few inches is acceptable to the fishes.

For three or four days the eggs remain above the surface and during this period the male periodically sprays water up on to the spawn to keep it moist. This he does by rapidly moving his tail just beneath the surface of the water underneath the eggs. The fry drop into the water on hatching, and at this stage the parents should be removed.

Another characin with an unusual spawning method is

female

A pair of Swordtail Characins (*top* and *bottom*)

the Swordtail Characin (*Corynopoma riisei*) and even now experts are not certain what actually takes place.

The male, apart from having extensions to some of its fins, including the lower part of the tail, has long filaments extending from the gill covers at the end of which are small discs. Normally these gill extensions lie flat along the body of the fish but when the courtship display takes place they are extended at right angles. How fertilization of the eggs takes place is a mystery as the fishes do not come together during spawning. They swim side by side a short distance apart and a few seconds later the female deposits eggs on a plant leaf. The whole process is repeated several times until about one hundred eggs are laid.

Whether internal fertilization takes place is not certain but it has been reported that females separated from males for some time have produced eggs which have hatched. Some breeders think that the male ejects sperm into the spoon-like discs on the gill filaments and then transfers this to the female. Others think that the female carries sperm in her mouth as she pecks at the leaves before depositing the eggs.

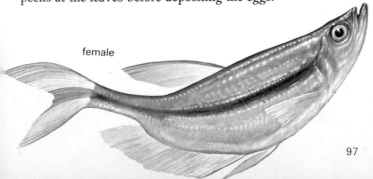

## Other members of the Characidae

The White or Spotted Piranha *(Serrasalmus rhombeus)*, the so-called 'terror of the Amazon', is reputed to be capable of stripping the flesh from a cow in a few minutes. It has extremely powerful and sharp teeth.

The Red Piranha *(Rooseveltiella nattereri)* grows to 12 inches in the wild. There are a number of genera to which the popular name piranha is given. A number of species have been kept and bred in aquaria in recent years, but in general only young fishes are suitable for private aquaria.

*Metynnis schreitmuelleri* is closely related to the piranhas but has completely different characteristics. It requires a mixed diet in the aquarium with some vegetable matter.

The X-ray Fish *(Pristella riddlei)* is attractive, easily bred and a fish every beginner should have. Males are distinguished by a white line on the leading edge of the anal fin.

White Piranha (1); *Metynnis schreitmuelleri* (2); Red Piranha (3); X-ray Fish (4)

*Nannostomus anomalus* is a small example of the pencil-fishes which is easily obtainable although not too popular. It does not display itself well in dealers' tanks, but retires to the shady corners it prefers. It is relatively easy to breed.

The Emperor Tetra *(Nematobrycon palmeri)* is one of the most beautiful introductions to Britain. The males are distinguished by tail extensions. It is not a prolific breeder.

The Congo Tetra *(Micralestes interruptus)* is one of the few

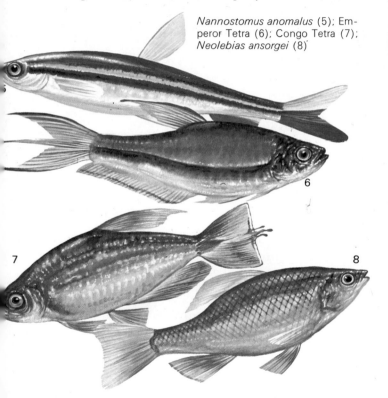

*Nannostomus anomalus* (5); Emperor Tetra (6); Congo Tetra (7); *Neolebias ansorgei* (8)

worth-while characins from Africa. It is rarely seen but worth purchasing should the opportunity arise.

The colours of *Neolebias ansorgei* really shine in the very soft acid water it prefers. It is easily bred but is a shy fish, tending to hide in vegetation.

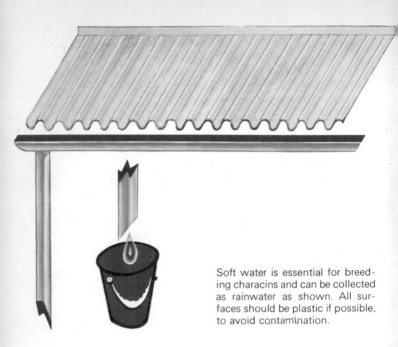

Soft water is essential for breeding characins and can be collected as rainwater as shown. All surfaces should be plastic if possible, to avoid contamination.

## Breeding characins

In most cases, breeding characins is much more of a problem than breeding barbs and danios. Generally speaking, however, characins spawn in the same manner as the barbs, in that the male courts the female and eventually both fishes come together side by side and fertilized eggs are released. Here the similarity ends. Characin eggs usually hatch more quickly and the fry are much smaller than those of the barbs. It is not unusual to have a pair of fishes spawn in the morning and to see the fry hatched later the same day. Of course, they are very poorly developed at first and will not require food for some days. Because they are smaller, the fry should be fed on infusoria for longer than is necessary for barbs although it is surprising how large the mouth of the fry is, in proportion to body size.

Water conditions are extremely important. A few species such as the Black Widow or Black Tetra *(Gymnocorymbus ternetzi)*, the Beacon Fish *(Hemigrammus ocellifer)* and the Black-line Tetra *(Hyphessobrycon scholzei)* can be persuaded to spawn in water with a hardness of 150–180 ppm and with pH on the alkaline side, but with the Neon Tetra *(Hyphesso-brycon innesi)* and some others the pH must be lower at about 6 but most important, the hardness must be below 15 ppm.

If tap water is soft, it is only necessary to leave it standing for a short while to allow any chlorine to dissipate. Hard tap water, however, must be 'softened'. This is best done by using ion exchange resins; one to remove the cations and one to remove the anions. This demineralized water should be mixed with small quantities of tap water to give the required hardness. For the aquarist with hard tap water the collection of rainwater is therefore a necessity. Rainwater collected in the country can be used within a few days. In towns, however, the rain has absorbed atmospheric impurities and these must be allowed to settle out or evaporate. It is a good idea to allow this rainwater to 'mature' over a layer of well-boiled peat.

The brilliantly coloured Neon Tetra is difficult to spawn

When breeding such fishes as the Zebra Danio, bright light acts as a stimulus to the fishes but with characins it has the reverse effect. It is therefore advisable to place the breeding tank where it will not receive strong light, and after the fishes have spawned, to cover the tank completely so that as little light as possible enters. It is possible that strong light produces either too much, or a special type of bacteria which attacks the eggs, but this is not certain. The breeding tank can have some of its faces painted to exclude light but this seems to have a claustrophobic effect on the fishes if a small aquarium is used. The water temperature should be around 80°F and a nylon spawning mop should be included as the eggs are adhesive or semi-adhesive.

Very often characins do not spawn on the day after they have been placed in the breeding tank and there is always a temptation to feed the fishes. This should not be done and fishes can generally last at least a week without being fed. Feeding results in uneaten food and more excreta, producing bacteria harmful to the eggs when the fishes do spawn.

Breeding tank with nylon mop suitable for the smaller characins. Painted sides help to exclude light.

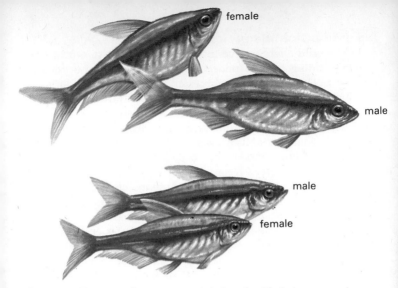

female

male

male

female

Glowlight Tetras perform an unusual barrel-roll' during spawning. During the movement, which takes place extremely quickly, the female moves over and around the male while releasing her eggs. The pair then separate and repeat the movement until spawning is complete.

It is impossible to exclude all bacteria as the breeding fishes are bound to produce some excreta while in the tank, but it is very important to keep the bacteria level to a minimum. If the spawning tank is well washed before setting up, the water well matured over peat and the spawning medium boiled before placing in the aquarium, then the conditions should be suitable.

The fry of the characins are also very light sensitive and when the eggs do hatch, the breeder should not be surprised if he sees nothing during the day. Quite a few eggs may turn white due to infertility, while the fry that hatch have a tendency to go into hiding. The best way to see if anything has happened is to wait until after dark and then shine a bright light into the tank from the side and look in from the top. The fry, which have by this time moved around the tank, immediately dive for cover. After a week or so, the fishes will be a little braver and will move into open water, but they are still very shy even at this stage.

## Family Cichlidae (cichlids)

In the wild, cichlids live in standing or sluggish water with good hiding places under overhanging banks or among plants. They take up definite territories, the boundaries of which are fiercely defended, and characteristic attack, defence and surrender postures have been well described. In groups of aquarium cichlids a hierarchy in order of aggressiveness often becomes established – a 'pecking order'.

Apart from *Tilapia* and *Geophagus* species, which are almost completely vegetarian, the cichlids are carnivorous and feed on smaller fishes and aquatic insects in their natural environment. Dried food will be eaten if nothing else is provided but minced liver, fish and cod roe are acceptable substitutes for live foods. A number of species enjoy digging up the gravel, thus uprooting plants and are therefore better kept in a tank set up specially for them. Though most cichlids are not particular about the *p*H or hardness of water most species do better if kept in soft, acid water.

Because of their relatively large size and quick growth under the right conditions, cichlids are used as food fishes in many tropical regions of the world. Young fishes are placed in rice paddies and then harvested when the rice is picked. (See page 5).

To breed cichlids it is often better to let eight to twelve young fishes grow up together and let them choose their own mates as they become sexually mature. There have been instances where the male has refused to mate with, and in

Distribution of the cichlids

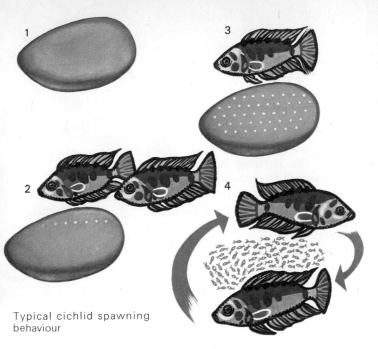

Typical cichlid spawning
behaviour

some cases even killed, an apparently perfect female newly introduced to the tank. In a typical spawning the partners select a flat stone or broad plant leaf and clean it to their satisfaction [1].

Dwarf cichlids need clean, clear, soft acid water with no gravel and find a plant-pot a good substitute for a flat stone. When courtship begins both fishes become vividly coloured. The female lays her eggs in regular rows on the stone, a few at a time, and these are immediately fertilized by the male [2]. Usually both parents then stand guard over the eggs, fanning them and picking out infertile ones [3]. When the eggs hatch, usually two days later, the fry are moved by the parents to another spot and guarded there until they are free swimming, usually in three to five days. Even then the fry are kept together in a shoal and protected by the parents [4]. In the mouth-breeders, the fertilized eggs are carried about in the mouth of one or other parent until the fry are free swimming.

About twenty of the sixty species of cichlids available to the aquarist are under 4 inches in length and are known as dwarf cichlids. More demanding in their needs than the larger cichlids, they must have soft acid water for spawning. The female usually looks after the brood after hatching and the male should be removed after spawning has taken place. One variety Agassiz's Dwarf Cichlid *(Apistogramma agassizi)* comes from the Amazon Basin.

Ramirez' Dwarf Cichlid *(Apistogramma ramirezi)* is a very beautiful fish. To keep it in its best condition the water must be soft and acid and absolutely clean.

The Golden-eyed Dwarf Cichlid *(Nannacara anomala)* comes from Guiana and is relatively easy to breed. After spawning the male should be removed. The female will then move the newly hatched fishes to a hollow in the gravel, where they become free swimming on the fifth day.

*Pelmatochromis kribensis* comes from West Africa and is one of the larger dwarf cichlids. These fishes are great diggers and will dig a pit in the gravel 2 inches deep and

Agassiz's Dwarf Cichlid

Ramirez' Dwarf Cichlid

Golden-eyed Dwarf Cichlid

*Pelmatochromis kribensis*

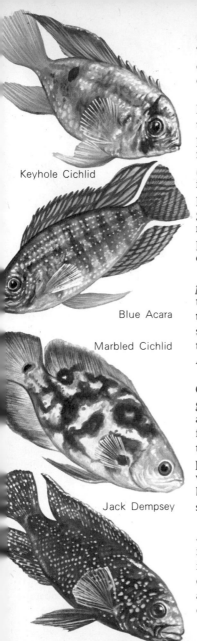

Keyhole Cichlid

Blue Acara

Marbled Cichlid

Jack Dempsey

3 inches across very easily. The broods often tend to contain many more fishes of one sex than the other.

Some members of the Cichlidae are not very popular as they grow large, grub up plants and need plenty of live foods. The Keyhole Cichlid *(Aequidens maroni)* however, is a peaceful fish in which parental care is usually very good. The sex difference is most easily seen in the more pointed dorsal and anal fins of the male.

The Blue Acara *(Aequidens pulcher)* although a very beautiful fish, grows too large for the average aquarist. The best specimens are to be seen in the large tanks of public Aquaria.

The Marbled or Velvet Cichlid *(Astronotus ocellatus)* grows to 13 inches but even at this size is a peaceful fellow. The young fishes up to 6 inches long, are much prettier than the adults, whose marbled effect is less bright and are more heavy in shape.

The Jack Dempsey *(Cichlasoma biocellatum)* is an aptly named fish. A predator growing to 8 inches in length, it is destructive to plants and not a suitable species for the community tank.

Fire-mouth Cichlid (1); Banded Cichlid (2); *Geophagus jurupari* (3); Pike Chichlid (4)

The Fire-mouth Cichlid *(Cichlasoma meeki)* is a popular cichlid probably because it is peaceful, well behaved and is easy to breed. A mature pair in good condition will often breed in the community tank, the parents taking it in turn to either guard the eggs, or patrolling to keep off intruders.

The Banded Cichlid *(Cichlasoma severum)* is another attractive cichlid to keep but it is more likely to dig up plants than is the Fire-mouth. This is an easy fish to breed once a pair decide they are compatible but the male may be possessive and behave aggressively towards strange females.

The Pike Cichlid *(Crenicichla lepidota)* is a predatory fish with a big mouth and because of its predatory nature requires a tank to itself.

*Geophagus jurupari,* sometimes called the Earth-eating Devilfish, is the most peaceful of the 'earth eaters' available to aquarists. The name 'earth eater' originates from the thorough way in which it digs up the bottom of the aquarium.

The Orange Chromide *(Etroplus maculatus)* comes from India and Ceylon, often from brackish water. Orange Chromides spawn in the usual cichlid manner and both parents look after the fry. Often, however, it is better to remove both parents and aerate the eggs artificially.

The Small or Egyptian Mouth-breeder *(Haplochromis multicolor)* is a popular aquarium fish. After spawning in excavations in the gravel the female takes all the eggs in her mouth where they hatch after ten days.

The Red or Jewel Cichlid *(Hemichromis bimaculatus)* is one of the most beautiful and interesting of cichlids. Often too robust for community tanks, they live quite well among their own kind. Spawning takes place on a flat stone with both fishes taking care of the eggs. The young need plenty of live food or much destructive fin biting will occur.

The Mozambique Cichlid or Mouth-brooder *(Tilapia mossambica)* is a representative of a large genus of cichlids from Africa; many of these fishes are used as foods. The eggs are laid in shallow depressions and are immediately taken into the mouth of the female and hatch after ten days.

Orange Chromide (5); Mozambique Cichlid (6); Small Mouth-breeder (7); Jewel Cichlid (8)

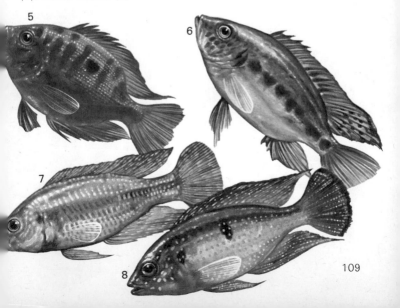

109

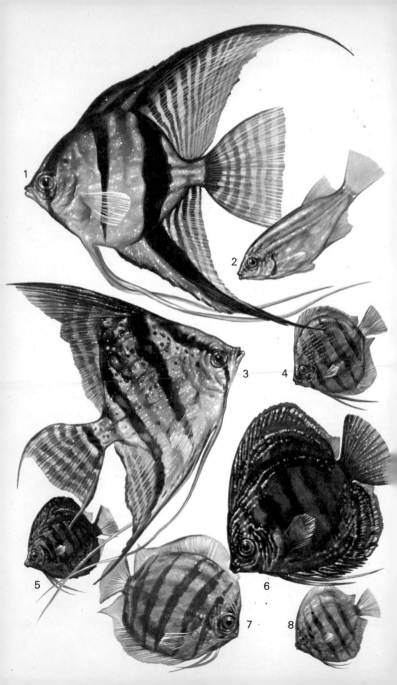

The angelfishes *(Pterophyllum* spp) are native to the Amazon and the Orinoco and the most popular of all cichlids. There are three species: *P. altum*, *P. eimekei* and *P. scalare* and the differences between them are recognizable only by the expert. Many of the 'angels' in fish tanks today are probably hybrids from the latter two species. They are peaceful fishes, very suitable for the community tank, but should not be kept below 74°F. They seem to do best in slightly acid water at a pH of 6·8.

Angelfishes are best left to choose mates for themselves. Once they have selected each other a pair will proceed to clean up one of the leaves of a broad-leafed plant, the eggs are then laid and looked after by both parents. Many aquarists prefer to let them spawn on a piece of slate, which is then removed and put near an aerator until the eggs hatch. Immature fishes are impossible to sex. They do, however, exhibit the typical cichlid, rather than angel shape, until they are three or four weeks old. Young fishes will eat powder-fine dried food but it is not as good for them as live food.

The Discus *(Symphysodon discus)* is a particularly spectacular aquarium fish, the breeding colours of which rival the gaudy beauty of most marine fishes. This is probably the fish most aquarists would like to be able to rear successfully. It is a difficult fish to keep and needs clean, very soft, acid water. It appears to do much better if the water is regularly filtered through a filter containing peat. All live foods are accepted by the Discus but when young fishes are first bought it is sometimes difficult to persuade them to feed.

Spawning takes place in the usual cichlid way on plant leaves or stones and both parents share in 'fanning' the eggs. The young hatch in about two days and are transferred to leaves onto which they hang for another two days before becoming free swimming. The parents at this stage appear to secrete a nutritious substance from the skin on which the young feed for a few days. With good care they grow rapidly to 3 or 4 inches in six months. Growth is then slow and it takes about two to three years for a fish to reach 6 inches.

Angelfishes (1, 3) with young (2), and Discus (5, 6) with colour varieties (4, 7, 8)

Spiny Catfish (1); Bronze Catfish (2); *Pimelodella* (3); Whiptail Catfish (4)

## Other interesting species

The Bronze Catfish *(Corydoras aeneus)* is the most common member of a very large genus from South America. All members have the same body shape but the body patterns vary quite a lot. Sizes range from $1\frac{1}{4}$ to $3\frac{1}{2}$ inches.

*Pimelodella gracilis* is another catfish from South America, with long whiskers. These fishes grow to at least 6 inches long and are therefore suitable for only the largest aquaria.

*Acanthodoras spinosissimus* is known as the Spiny or Talking Catfish, the latter because it makes a croaking noise at times. It is not a pretty fish. Its fins are very stiff and spiny and it grows to at least 5 inches.

The Whiptail Catfish *(Loricaria parva)* with its long, thin tail is aptly named. This is one of the catfishes which likes algae in its diet and it is therefore a useful fish for cleaning algae from rocks and glass in the aquarium. It has been successfully bred in captivity.

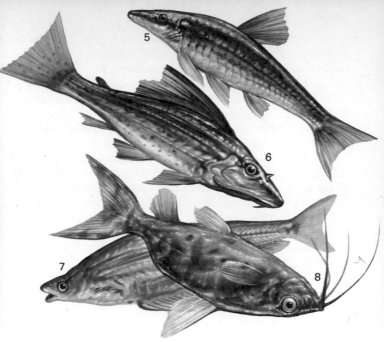

*Otocinclus vittatus* (5); *Plecostomus commersoni* (6); Glass Catfish (7); Upside-down Catfish (8)

*Otocinclus vittatus* is one of the more commonly seen algae eaters. Because of its size its appetite is not very large and it should not be expected to clear too much algae. It grows to only 2 inches long.

In contrast, *Plecostomus commersoni* will eat all the algae that can be provided, usually growing too big for the tank in the process. In nature it grows to well over a foot long but fortunately does not reach that length in an aquarium. Because of its size it can damage plants when resting on them.

The Glass Catfish *(Kryptopterus bicirrhis)* is one of the most transparent fish seen in aquaria. Not really a scavenger like most catfishes, it prefers live foods.

The Upside-down Catfish *(Synodontis nigriventris)* has the habit of swimming in an upside-down position for a while, returning to normal when at rest. There are one or two other species in the genus all of which have this peculiar habit.

The Kuhli Loach *(Acanthophthalmus kuhlii)* is common in most dealers' tanks spending its time hiding in corners and under rocks. It moves very quickly, especially when a net comes close to it. It is an excellent scavenger.

The Clown Loach or Tiger Botia *(Botia macracantha)* is the most beautiful species of this genus. Not often seen, it is always expensive. Other species are imported from time to time and all make good scavengers.

*Gyrinocheilus aymonieri* is one of the most useful fishes for the aquarist and nearly every tank should have one. It eats all the algae on the glass and plant leaves and does not grow too big. It has replaced *Plecostomus commersoni* as the most popular aquarium cleaner (see page 147).

*Noemacheilus fasciatus* is a little loach more interesting than the Kuhli Loach as it does not hide away so much. It is another excellent scavenger.

The Dwarf Rainbowfish *(Melanotaenia maccullochi)* is the

Kuhli Loach (1); Clown Loach (2); *Gyrinocheilus aymonieri* (3); *Noemacheilus fasciatus* (4)

most common member of the group of Australian rainbows. Interesting features are a double dorsal fin and the fact that they do not eat their eggs and can, therefore, be spawned very easily.

The Black-banded Sunfish *(Mesogonistius chaetodon)* is a native of the United States and does not like temperatures much in excess of 70°F. It does not like dried foods and therefore can be difficult to keep.

The Malayan Angel or Fingerfish *(Mondactylus argenteus)* is one of the few fishes kept in tropical aquaria which is really a brackish-water fish. As such, they appreciate some salt added to the water. They are rather shy fishes and should be kept in a shoal if possible.

The Scat or Argus *(Scatophagus argus)* is similar to the previous species and inhabits the same waters. Scats look attractive in a tank with Malayan Angels and will eat all foods in huge quantities including aquarium plants.

Dwarf Rainbowfish (5); Malayan Angel (6); Black-banded Sunfish (7); Scat (8)

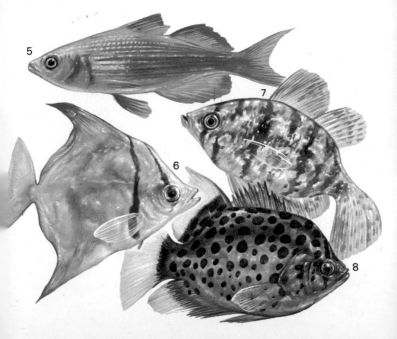

The Spiny Eel *(Mastacembelus maculatus)* has a habit of burying itself in the gravel with only its eyes and snout showing. It is extremely difficult to catch when in the aquarium and is not really a fish for the community tank.

The Glassfish *(Chanda lala)* has a near transparent body and is quite hardy. It prefers hard water and live foods although it will accept some dried foods. It is not easily bred and requires shallow water and plenty of plants.

The Butterfly-fish *(Pantodon buchholzi)*, so named because of its large pectoral fins, has an enormous mouth and takes only live foods, mainly insects, at the surface. This is a freshwater flying fish, and is said to skim along the surface for distances up to six feet.

The Mudskipper *(Periophthalmus barbarus)* can and does spend a large part of its life out of water. When submerged it uses its extended eyes to look above the water before emerging. The pectoral fins are used as feet and strong muscles enable these fishes to move quite quickly when suddenly alarmed.

Spiny Eel (1); Glassfish (2); Butterfly-fish (3); Mudskipper (4)

The Common Puffer-fish *(Tetraodon cutcutia)* is a fish well known for its habit of inflating itself when alarmed. If the fish is taken from water it usually performs this feat and remains floating upside-down for a few moments before deflating. These fishes require some salt added to their aquarium, and will eat most food. In the wild they are scavengers.

The Bumblebee-fish *(Brachygobious xanthozona)* also appreciates a little salt in its water. These are timid fishes and should be given a tank to themselves as they are slow to get to food. They will only eat live foods.

The African Knifefish *(Xenomystus nigri)* has no dorsal or caudal fins and swims by a rippling motion of the anal fin. It requires live food and is not a community fish.

The Archerfish *(Toxotes jaculator)* has a special mouth structure which enables it to expel small drops of water at insects on foliage, 3 or 4 feet above the surface. It does this with extreme accuracy. This fish requires live food in the aquarium.

Common Puffer-fish (5); Bumble-bee-fish (6); African Knifefish (7); Archerfish (8)

Although not the kind of fishes every aquarist would want to keep, lung-fishes are biologically very interesting. They are 'living fossils' and their ancient ancestors were the forbears of the amphibians 300 million years ago.

The primitive lungs of these fishes enable them to breathe air, which is of great value in the dry season. Some species bury themselves in the mud as soon as the water dries up, forming a cocoon which keeps the fish moist. A hole at the mouth end of the cocoon allows the fish to breathe. This summer sleep ceases when the rains begin, the pools fill with water and the fishes emerge from their cocoons. Other species of lung-fishes do not build cocoons but can live in small stagnant pools, breathing air to prevent asphyxiation.

In aquaria, lung-fishes always appear to be uninteresting, sluggish fishes, sitting on the bottom of the tank. They eat fishes, earthworms, meat, snails and mussels. All species are capable of giving a nasty bite so must be handled with care. In the wild, breeding takes place at the beginning of the rainy season and the eggs are said to be large and yolky, rather like amphibian eggs. Most public Aquaria usually have at least one specimen of these unusual fishes.

South American (1), African (2)
and Australian (3) lungfishes

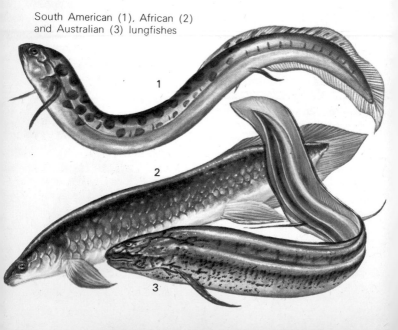

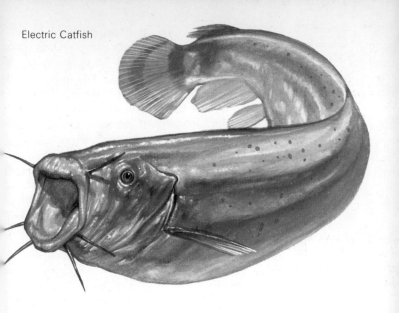

Mention must be made of two individual fishes that are also more suitable for the public rather than the private aquarium. At the time of writing the first of these can be seen in the Aquarium of the London Zoo at Regents Park.

The first fish is the Electric Catfish *(Malapterurus electricus)* which comes from Africa and as its name suggests is capable of discharging an electric current. As it grows to around 2 feet in length and lives exclusively on small, live fishes few aquariums are equipped to keep this fish. In the London Zoo Aquarium, the tank contains electrical equipment to detect the discharges made by the fish. The results can be heard as a crackling noise on a loudspeaker.

The second unusual fish is *Arapaima gigas* (see page 7). Until recently the London Zoo had a specimen which was at least 5 feet long and a really beautiful fish. It glided majestically around its tank by slight movements of the tail, paying no attention at all to other fishes. Because of its shape, the Arapaima can move very fast when required. In the Amazon region this fish forms an important part of the diet of natives who dry the flesh and preserve it for future meals.

# FOODS AND FEEDING

All foodstuffs consist of varying amounts of the following substances: proteins, fats, carbohydrates, vitamins and mineral substances. Proteins, fats and carbohydrates are all capable of being used by the fish to give it energy, though fats have twice the calorific value of proteins and carbohydrates. Proteins are complex substances made up of amino acids. Some of these can be manufactured from other amino acids but other essential amino acids must come from the food directly, i.e., they cannot be manufactured by the fish. Similarly, some of the fatty acids of which fats are composed cannot be manufactured from other fats by the fish, and must be taken in as part of the diet. Vitamins are essential for growth and health and supplies of minerals such as calcium, phosphorus and iodine must also be adequate, to prevent ill health and stunted growth.

To ensure healthy growth, therefore, the fishes must have a mixed and balanced diet containing both dried food and various live foods such as Whiteworm, *Tubifex*, *Daphnia*, earthworms and mosquito larvae. If there are algae or plants in the tank for the fishes to eat, so much the better. This diet can be supplemented by protein foods such as liver, beef and heart to provide variety.

It must also be remembered that fishes find some foods much more interesting than others, as do humans. Most fishes, for example, would prefer to have their protein allowance in the form of living mosquito larvae rather than pieces of cooked liver. Change helps to avoid boredom from one type of food however.

There are some species which are more specialized in the way they like to take in their nutriment, the predators, for example, preferring living fishes and insects and others preferring mainly plant food.

Of great use to the aquarist are the commercially prepared dried foods, generally consisting of a mixture of cereal, milk powder, prepared egg, dried *Daphnia*, shrimp or fish. These are dried and mixed together and presented as a fine power or as flakes. Others have various chemicals added which are reputed to give colour to the fishes. The aquarist can prepare

Meat for aquarium fishes can be shredded in a Mouli Blender

his own dry food, some for example, grind down proprietary cat food to various sized particles. Others use various cereals, especially those in a flakey form prepared for babies and our own experience is that these are very good. It is important to give dried foods in small quantities — no more than can be eaten by the fishes in ten minutes. Any residue putrifies and will pollute the tank. More fishes have died from this form of over feeding than from under feeding.

Fishes can be given small pieces of cooked, flaked fish (especially when food is scarce in winter), shrimps and small amounts of tinned salmon. Liver is a particularly good food, it is high in protein, contains vitamins and is rich in iron. Raw liver, however, tends to make the tank cloudy and to avoid this it should be put in boiling water for a few minutes, to coagulate the blood. The liver should then be cut into small cubes and shredded, in a blender if one is available. To improve this food, shrimps can be shredded up in the blender or cooked cod roe, and the whole lot mixed together.

Another useful food is a hard-boiled egg with the white removed. The yolk can be frozen in the refrigerator and bits sliced off when needed. From time to time fishes also like a pinch of wheatgerm. This contains large amounts of vitamin B and is very much liked by mollies.

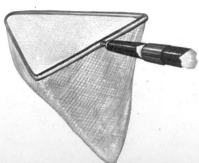

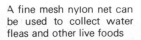

A fine mesh nylon net can be used to collect water fleas and other live foods

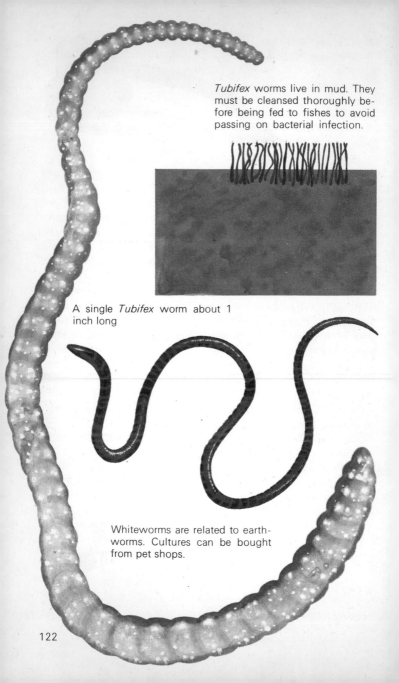

*Tubifex* worms live in mud. They must be cleansed thoroughly before being fed to fishes to avoid passing on bacterial infection.

A single *Tubifex* worm about 1 inch long

Whiteworms are related to earthworms. Cultures can be bought from pet shops.

## Whiteworms

The Whiteworm *(Enchytraeus albidus)* is one of the live foods that can be cultivated by the aquarist and so is available all the year round. To get a culture growing successfully a wooden box is required with provision for water to escape when the culture media is watered. Special culture media can be bought or mixtures of soil, peat and fine sand prepared at home, and sterilized by heat before use.

The worm culture is added to the moist culture medium and the food placed in a small hollow on top of the medium. A piece of glass is usually placed over the box and finally a lid. The box should be kept in the dark at about 55°F. The worms usually come up to the surface, eat the food and cling to the glass. They can easily be lifted off with forceps and fed to the fishes.

Food for Whiteworms can be bought ready prepared, or alternatively baby cereal food can be used. After three days any unused food should be removed and the whole culture medium stirred. This breaks up the medium, aerates it and certainly improves the culture. Fishes should not be fed Whiteworms exclusively as they have a high fat content and can cause obesity.

## Tubifex

*Tubifex* worms live at the bottom of streams and rivers, particularly where large amounts of organic matter are present, as in polluted water. They have their front end buried in the mud and the rear end constantly waving in the water. If these worms are collected directly from a river it is difficult to avoid also collecting smelly mud and the worms take a lot of cleaning. It is, therefore, preferable to buy *Tubifex* from pet shops where they are already clean. Even so the gut of the worm usually contains much organic matter and bacteria, and so the worms must be well washed for forty-eight hours before being fed to the fishes. They are best placed in a bowl left under a running tap.

Because they are aquatic, *Tubifex* will continue to live in the gravel at the bottom of the tank if not eaten. They are very nutritious and well liked by all fishes. A recent development is freeze-dried *Tubifex* available from pet shops.

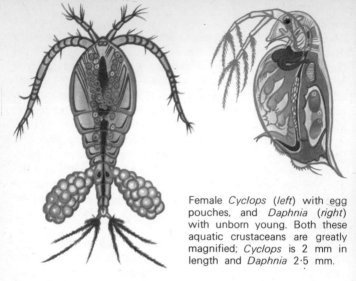

Female *Cyclops* (*left*) with egg pouches, and *Daphnia* (*right*) with unborn young. Both these aquatic crustaceans are greatly magnified; *Cyclops* is 2 mm in length and *Daphnia* 2·5 mm.

## Water fleas

Water fleas form a large group of crustaceans living in ponds; the best known being *Daphnia* and *Cyclops*. These small creatures use their swimming antennae to move jerkily about in the water and this is probably how the name 'flea' originated. They can be found in large numbers during the warm months of the year especially if the pond contains rotting organic matter. Farm-yard ponds are often very good sources of supply and the fleas should be caught using a fine-mesh net and fed quickly to the fishes. During summer many young, usually females, are produced, but as the weather gets cooler specially resistant eggs are produced which survive the winter.

*Daphnia* have a laxative property because they feed predominantly on algae from which they obtain oil. They are therefore a very good food for fishes kept in the confined space of an aquarium. It is wise not to overfeed, however, as a surfeit can kill fishes and may even pollute the tank.

## Other live foods

Gnat or mosquito larvae are the larvae of *Culex pipiens* and are often found in enormous numbers on the surface of stagnant waters. Easily caught in summer when catching

*Daphnia*, they are a nuisance because those uneaten hatch out as gnats in the fish house. Tooth-carps are particularly partial to gnat larvae and some live-bearers have been used in mosquito control.

Bloodworms are the larvae of the midge *Chironomus plumosus*. They occur in large numbers in ponds and ditches receiving organic matter. If required in large numbers, mud from the upper layer of the pond bottom should be sieved through a small sieve.

Glass or Phantom larvae are the transparent larvae of the fly *Corethra plumicornis*. They survive the winter in sheltered ponds. An excellent food, they are very hardy but should not be given alive to small fishes because they have been known to eat spawn and newly hatched fry. They can given chopped or squashed for young fishes.

The Freshwater Shrimp *(Gammarus pulex)* can be a useful food for larger fishes as it grows to nearly an inch in length. Shrimps are often found under stones or among water plants in running water.

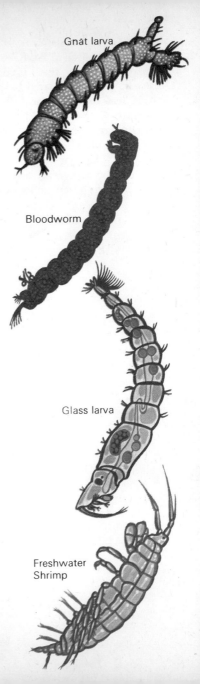

Gnat larva

Bloodworm

Glass larva

Freshwater Shrimp

Examples of live foods for fishes (magnified)

## Foods for fry

Many newly hatched fry have very small mouths and consequently need very small food, for the first few days of life. Infusoria can be prepared by adding a small piece of bruised lettuce leaf to a jam-jar full of water. A small amount of aquarium water should be added to this and the mixture incubated at 76°F for forty-eight hours. The protozoa added with the tank water feed on the rotting lettuce leaf and multiply. A half jar twice a day of such infusoria should be sufficient for an average sized aquarium.

Water from green tanks or ponds contains either *Euglena*

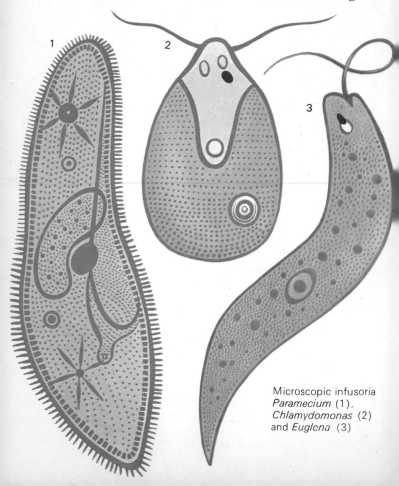

Microscopic infusoria
*Paramecium* (1),
*Chlamydomonas* (2)
and *Euglena* (3)

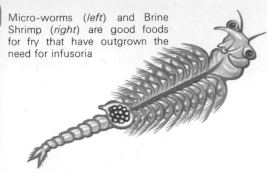

Micro-worms (*left*) and Brine Shrimp (*right*) are good foods for fry that have outgrown the need for infusoria

or *Chlamydomonas*, both excellent fry foods, which can also be cultured artificially. Newly hatched fry can also be fed on commercially available food which is easy to use. Another infusoria substitute is hard-boiled egg yolk which produces a cloud of very small nutritious particles in the breeding tank.

The Brine Shrimp *(Artemia salina)* is an important food for newly hatched fry with larger mouths. Brine Shrimp eggs are obtainable from most pet shops and can be hatched within forty-eight hours in a salt solution (two level teaspoonsfuls per pint of water) at 80°F. Using two or three jam-jars it is easy to organize a supply of newly hatched shrimps which can be filtered off through a very fine piece of cloth and rinsed into the tank.

Micro-worms *(Anguilluda silusia)* are small nematode worms only a fraction of an inch long. An initial culture must be obtained from another aquarist or pet shop. The culture medium consists of a one inch layer of cooked oatmeal porridge which has been allowed to cool in a 4 inch diameter plastic dish. The culture should be placed on top of this layer and a lid placed over the dish before incubation at 70–80°F. The worms multiply rapidly and swarm up the sides of the box from which they can be removed with a small brush. The culture goes sour after a time and must be replaced by inoculating some new medium from the old culture.

Grindal worms *(Enchytraeus buchholtzi)* are similar to White-worms and very useful for feeding growing fry, as they grow to only $\frac{3}{8}$ inch long. Cultures of grindal worms can be bought from most dealers and pet shops.

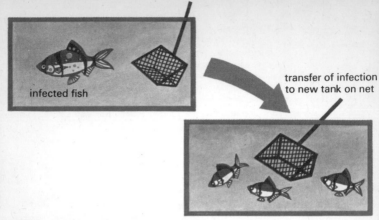

transfer of infection to new tank on net

infected fishes

It is easy to spread infectious disease from tank to tank. Quarantine tank equipment should never be used in other tanks.

## DISEASES OF FISHES

Fishes, like all animals, are subject to diseases, the most serious of which are infectious, as these can wipe out a great many fishes. Such diseases can, however, be cured but prevention is a far better course of action.

Congenital diseases are diseases or deformities with which the fish is born, examples being missing gill covers and fins or twisted backbones. These deformities are usually genetic in origin and one should not use parents or their offspring for breeding again.

Traumatic diseases are produced by injuries, usually caused by other fishes during fights, or sometimes when the fishes jump out on being netted.

Infectious diseases are tremendously common in fish tanks and are caused by protozoa, bacteria or viruses. Diseases caused by protozoa are the most common and the ones we know most about. All infectious diseases are introduced into a tank from another infected fish either directly, or by transferring the infection via a net. Many infectious diseases do not show at all in the early stages of development. The protozoa may be present on the fish but the characteristic lesion often does not develop. It can take up to six weeks before the illness becomes apparent, by which time other fishes in the tank will have become infected.

Aquarists with only one tank rely on the source from which they get their fishes being free of infection. Aquarists with several tanks should always have a quarantine tank with its own nets, feeding forceps, etc., which should never be used in other tanks. New fishes, after a quarantine of six weeks, should be carefully examined in a good light before being placed with healthy fishes.

Degenerative diseases are often caused by increasing age and fishes develop heart failure, kidney failure which leads to dropsy, skeletal deformities, swim bladder and balance troubles. Neoplastic disease, namely cancers due to new growth and pigmented tumours, are not unknown in fishes.

Healthy fishes are easily recognized. They feed well, the fins are erect, they are active, their colour is good and there are no spots or blemishes on the skin. Their eyes are bright and their gills pink. There are no skeletal deformities and the body cavity of the fish is not swollen or the belly hollow.

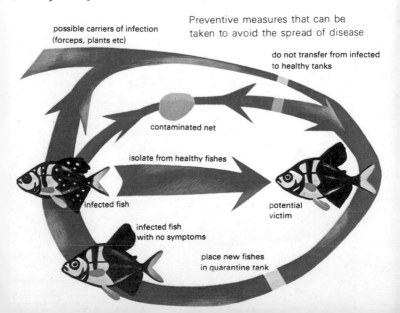

possible carriers of infection (forceps, plants etc)

Preventive measures that can be taken to avoid the spread of disease

do not transfer from infected to healthy tanks

contaminated net

isolate from healthy fishes

infected fish

potential victim

infected fish with no symptoms

place new fishes in quarantine tank

## White Spot disease

This is the most common infectious disease seen in tropical aquaria and will kill fishes if not checked. It is caused by a protozoan parasite *Ichthyophthirius multifilius*, and attacks are often caused by a drop in temperature of the aquarium water. The resistance of the fishes becomes reduced and the vitality of the parasite increased. Diagnosis is not easy in the early stages of the disease when only one spot may be present on one fish. However, the parasite appears to cause an itching in infected fishes and in the early stages, fishes may attempt to rub or scratch themselves against objects in the aquarium to reduce the irritation. The spots usually spread rapidly over a few days. As the life cycle of the parasite is known, control is not difficult.

The first step is to raise the water temperature to 82°F. This speeds up the development of the cysts to the free-living form, the stage at which a White Spot preparation will kill the parasite. Such preparations are commercially prepared and sold at most pet shops. Instructions on the direction circular must be carefully followed.

Alternatively the disease can be cured using a five per cent aqueous solution of methylene blue, available from all pharmacists. This is a very valuable substance to the aquarist as it also cures other diseases. Unfortunately, it harms plants so the fishes must be put in an unplanted tank, in which they

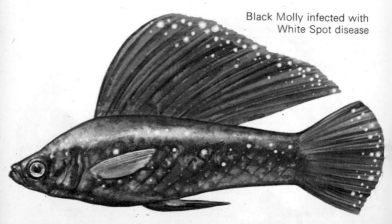

Black Molly infected with
White Spot disease

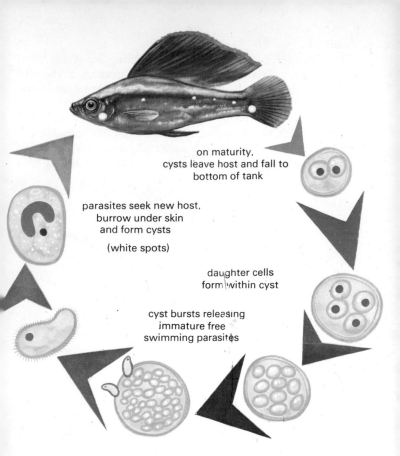

on maturity,
cysts leave host and fall to
bottom of tank

parasites seek new host,
burrow under skin
and form cysts

(white spots)

daughter cells
form within cyst

cyst bursts releasing
immature free
swimming parasites

Life cycle of the White Spot parasite

must be kept for ten days. If the blue colour of the water fades more methylene blue should be added. The planted tank, without fishes, will become free of parasites in ten days without any treatment.

If an outbreak of White Spot disease occurs in a community tank, only certain species may become infected, due to several reasons. The parasite prefers certain species as hosts, some species can withstand chilling better than others, and certain fishes in the aquarium will be in better health than others.

## Velvet

This is a comparatively new disease among aquarium fishes and affects mostly labyrinth fishes and members of the carp family such as the White Cloud Mountain Minnows, danios, barbs and also the live-bearing tooth-carps. Fishes with Velvet disease have golden dust-like spots on their skin as if sprayed with golden powder. If untreated, the condition of the fishes deteriorates and a series of raised circular crusts develops. This condition is caused by the free-swimming form

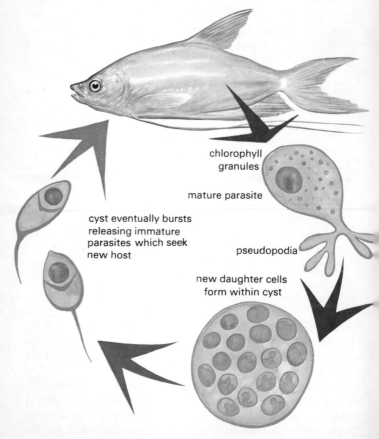

chlorophyll granules

mature parasite

cyst eventually bursts releasing immature parasites which seek new host

pseudopodia

new daughter cells form within cyst

Life cycle of the Velvet parasite

of *Oodinium limneticum* which adheres to the fish and grows pseudopodia into its skin to obtain nourishment. An infection usually kills young fishes and fry usually succumb before the disease is suspected. The free-swimming form contains chlorophyll and can therefore exist for a long time in the presence of light without requiring a fish host. This means that it is a much more difficult parasite to get rid of than *Ichthyophthirius*.

All fishes from the tank containing obviously infected fishes must be put in an isolation tank and treated with methylene blue for ten days, as for White Spot. Acriflavine (1/60 grain per gallon) can also be used but this drug can

White Cloud Mountain Minnow infected with Velvet disease. This species and other members of the carp family are particularly susceptible to the disease.

produce a temporary sterility in fishes. The original tank must also be sterilized and the plants removed and washed in a solution of potassium permanganate. The gravel should be washed and preferably stood for ten minutes in boiling water. The water from the tank must be discarded and the inside well rinsed with a weak solution of disinfectant detergent before a final rinse with fresh water. If this cleaning is not done further outbreaks of Velvet will continually occur in the infected tank. The cure should be effective in a few days but a second treatment can be repeated in five or six days.

We believe that every introduction of this disease into aquarists' tanks is from infected fishes, or from the water in which they were contained.

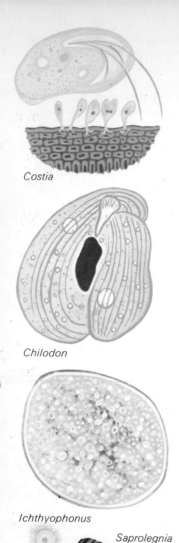

Costia

Chilodon

Ichthyophonus

Saprolegnia

## Other diseases and enemies

Costiasis is caused by a proto-zoan parasite *Costia necatrix* which grows in the mucus on the skin of fishes. The fishes become very lethargic with no appetite and respire rapid-ly. Fishes can be cured by putting them in two-and-a-half per cent salt water solu-tion for fifteen minutes every day.

The protozoan *Chilodon cyprini* attaches itself to both the gills and skin of the fish. The fish closes its dorsal and anal fins and often spirals up to the surface to grasp a bubble of air. Methylene blue or acriflavin are cures.

*Ichthyophonus hoferi* is a widely distributed species of fungi and probably the cause of many unidentified deaths in fishes. The illustration shows a section through a cyst from a fish's liver. The fungus grows through the intestinal lining and dissem-inates throughout the body. All infected fishes should be removed and destroyed.

*Saprolegnia* fungi are pres-ent in all aquarium waters but only attack fishes where damage to skin has occurred. The parasite grows at the skin wound producing a cot-ton wool-like growth but mycelia eventually invade the body tissues. Contaminated fishes should be removed and the wound painted daily with five per cent methylene blue.

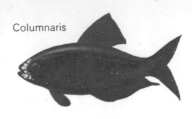
Columnaris

Columnaris disease is caused by a bacterial infection *Chondococus columnaris*. This usually enters the body through injured areas, generally near the mouth and a fungus-like growth develops. One 250 mg capsule of chloramphenicol per gallon usually effects a cure.

Fin rot

Fin rot is a bacterial infection of the fins. Entry is gained through a damaged fin and inflammation and destruction of fin tissues takes place. The disease can spread into the body and cause death. A weak solution of acriflavin or penicillin (1/60 grain per gallon) will cure.

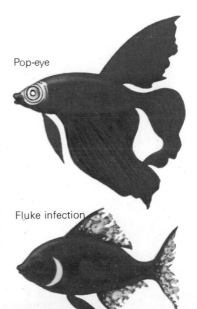
Pop-eye

Pop-eye exophthalmos is commonly seen in Siamese Fighting Fishes in which one eye becomes cloudy, swells and will lose its sight if not treated. The fish should be put in a net and one drop of organic silver eye drops applied four times a day.

Fluke infection

Fluke infections are caused by trematode worms. Of these, *Gyrodactylus* species grow on the body and *Dactylogyrus* species on the gills. An infected fish becomes pale,

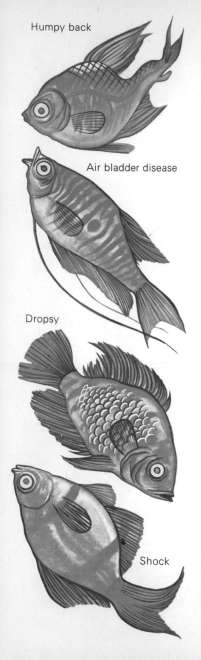

Humpy back

Air bladder disease

Dropsy

Shock

with wide open pale gills and torn and slimy fins. The fish should be kept in a deep blue solution of methylene blue for three days.

Senile changes occur in fishes just as in other animals when they become old. They become incapable of breeding, often lose a lot of their colour and develop deformities. A humpy back and air bladder disease are common among old fishes. Air bladder disease causes the fish to lose its ability to balance. It is suggested that infection, incorrect feeding, indigestion and low water temperatures can cause this trouble.

Dropsy is a disease in which the cavities of the body accumulate fluids until the scales tend to stick out at right angles. There is evidence that this is a virus infection but 250 mg of chloramphenicol per gallon added to the water, will usually cure. When only a single fish develops this disease it does not normally spread.

Fishes are vulnerable to sudden shocks. If tetras for example are transferred from acid to hard alkaline water they will turn over and perhaps die. Fishes placed in water of a different temperature will also show shock symptoms and fishes chased by the net when being caught may roll over on their backs and look very ill.

Among the enemies of fishes are hydras, small coelenterates living in fresh-water ponds. They feed mainly on water fleas which they first paralyse and then ingest. Hydras are quite capable of killing small fishes up to half an inch long. If a tank gets infected with hydras a few hungry guppies or gouramis will soon clear them up if they have no other food.

Hydras

Great Diving Beetle

Dragonfly larva

Piscicola

The Great Diving Beetle (*Dytiscus marginalis*) is present in many of the ponds which contain water fleas and therefore its larval form is likely to be caught in catches of *Daphnia*. The larva has large jaws through which it injects digestive juices before sucking up its victims' tissues. It can kill fishes larger than itself, using this method.

Dragonflies lay their eggs in water and the larvae are very voracious and will kill fishes larger than themselves. Any caught with *Daphnia* should be removed.

*Piscicola geomatra* is a fresh-water leech that will attack fishes. Other leeches found in ponds will attack only mammals, amphibians or snails.

Sediment settles out down the slope of the gravel

# SETTING UP THE HOME AQUARIUM

Setting up an aquarium in the home must be a carefully thought out operation. First of all thought must be given to where the tank is to go, remembering weight, size, amount of daylight, etc. Tanks to be built into alcoves need even more thought. There should be enough room above the tank for servicing, and the tank should be capable of being moved fairly easily if necessary. A plug for the electricity supply to carry heater, thermostats, lighting, and provision for working an air pump is needed. Electricity and water are a dangerous combination, so all electrical work should be done properly. It is also a good idea to conceal wires, connections and plugs or these will detract from the appearance of the tank.

Cost must obviously determine tank size but for a community tank 24 × 12 × 12 inches is the minimum size to set up an 'aquascape'. It is well worth spending extra on the tank and equipment in the beginning, as fishes can be gradually added later. Second-hand tanks should be bought with care, particularly if they have been stored dry for a considerable length of time. They tend to leak when filled with water and leaks are difficult to stop. Nevertheless, all tanks, whether new or second-hand should be put outside, filled with water and left for one week as a test. This week can be utilized for preliminary tasks, such as the preparation of the gravel. All aquarium composts, no matter how well washed they are reputed to be, always need additional washing.

When gravel is put into the tank it must always slope from back to front to allow detritus and sediment to settle to the front glass, from where it is easy to siphon off (see page 146).

Before adding the water it is advisable to place a layer of newspaper on the gravel. This prevents the water disturbing

Flow diagram to show stages in setting up an aquarium

19. Add fishes

6. Fill tank, leave outside for a week and check for leaks

5. Treatment of top of frame to prevent rust

7. Wash gravel

4. Purchase of tank, stand, cover, heater, thermostat, thermometer and gravel

18. Leave tank for one week, daily checking temperature and watching for leaks

8. Wash tank inside and out and wash gravel again

3. Comparison of tanks, frames available

17. Add cover and check lights

9. Add gravel to tank

16. Switch on

10. Add heater and thermostat and connect to each other but not to mains

2. Examination of established aquaria for ideas

15. Connect heating system to mains

14. Fill tank completely

11. Add rocks

1. Considerations of purpose, site, size, cost and contents

13. Add plants

12. Half fill tank with water

Add the water carefully over newspaper to avoid disturbing the gravel

the gravel and causing clouding. Water should be added at about 70°F, and when the tank is half full the rocks can be added. Rocks composed of limestone, marble, etc., should not be used as these will make the water very alkaline and cloudy. Granite and sandstone are very good rocks for aquaria but they must be well washed before they are placed in the tank.

Rockwork can be bought at pet shops, artificial rockwork can be made out of concrete, or the aquarist can collect

Red shale makes attractive aquarium rock work

natural rocks for his aquarium. There is no doubt that the latter produce the most beautiful effect. Concrete 'rockwork' must be well cured before use in the aquarium or the water is made very alkaline and will harm the fishes. The shape, size and colour of rock placed in the tank depends on the artistic abilities of the aquarist, but it must blend in with the gravel and plants. Generally, tall pieces are placed at the back and small pieces at the front. Community tanks set up at national shows will give the aquarist ideas of what to aim for.

The heater and thermostat are placed at opposite corners of the tank, the heater inclined at an angle and the thermostat vertical. If these two are placed near each other, cold pockets in the aquarium will be produced. There are very often layers of different temperatures in the aquarium, the bottom being a few degrees cooler than the surface. This is due somewhat to the bulb lighting the aquarium as this also heats the surface of the water. The thermometer is best positioned on the front glass on the same side as the thermostat, with its bulb in the middle of the tank.

Small fluctuations in temperature will not harm the fishes and in fact a slightly varying temperature is preferable to an exactly constant one. However, sudden changes will result in losses of fishes and once the tank is set up it is as well to check the temperature daily.

Thermostat and heater positions for even temperature

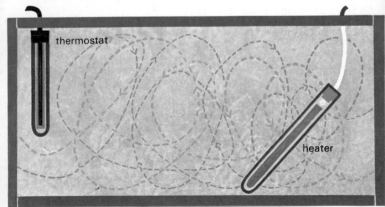

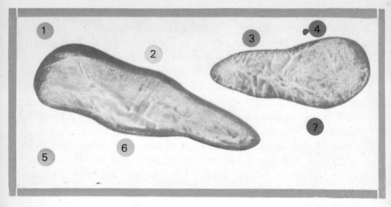

Suggested plan (*above*) and side view showing species (*opposite*) of a community tank planting. Species are *Ech. paniculatus* (1); *Crypt.*

Plants are best added to the aquarium when it is only half full. Planting sticks may be used and are a great help when putting in the last few plants. It is advisable not to lead down plants as lead in soft water produces lead hydroxide, which is poisonous. The plant roots should be pushed into the gravel as deep as the crown of the plant but must be handled delicately. The variety of plants used and how many, depends upon the taste of the aquarist. It is important not to over-plant, because the plants will grow and soon become over-crowded if there were too many planted initially.

For community tanks some aquarists prefer mixtures of cryptocorynes with a little *Sagittaria* but others have different preferences. Plants like Indian Fern and Giant Hygrophila often grow tremendously quickly but cryptocorynes grow slowly so that a reasonably stable environment is presented. Floating plants do very poorly in the community aquarium indoors because heat from the electric light bulbs in the tank cover scorch them. They also block light from the other plants and thus have no place in the indoor community tank.

Once all the plants are in, the tank can be completely filled. It is advisable to do this using a watering can with a rose attachment. An occasional plant may float during this procedure but can be replanted with planting sticks without too

*affinis* (2); *Crypt. becketti* (3); *Cabomba* (4); *Bacopa* (5); *Crypt. nevelli* (6); and *Ech. tenellis* (7).

much difficulty. It takes a little time for the plants to establish themselves and the week allowed to stabilize temperatures and check leaks before the fishes are put in gives the plants time to settle down and begin to root. During early stages of the life of a new tank algae may appear as they have at this stage no competition from the higher plants. This algae is best controlled by cutting down the light temporarily.

Razor blade glass scraper (*top*) and planting stick (*bottom*)

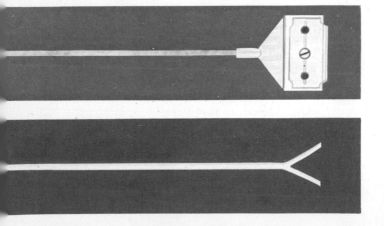

Suggested guide to the surface area requirements of fishes based on their ultimate size

| Fish | Maximum size (ins) | Surface area required per fish (sq. ins) |
|---|---|---|
| guppy | 2 | 5 |
| neon | 2 | 5 |
| swordtail | 3 | 20 |
| platy | 3 | 20 |
| fighter | 3 | 20 |
| Gyrinocheilus | 3 | 20 |
| barb | $3\frac{1}{2}$ | 30 |
| cichlid | 5 | 60 |

For example, a 24 x 12 x 12 inch tank (surface area 288 sq. inches) would hold, assuming they were of maximum size, six guppies, one angel, six swordtails, two barbs and one Gyrinocheilus—a total surface area requirement of 290 sq. inches.

Once the tank has been working properly for a week the fishes can be bought. The selection depends upon the taste of the aquarist but for a complete beginner fishes should be selected from the following species: guppies, swordtails, platies, smaller barbs, mollies, tetras, Zebra Danios and one Gyrinocheilus aymonieri. These are all colourful fishes and will live together peacefully. One male Siamese Fighting Fish can be added to provide a dash of colour and a talking point. Angelfishes, if added, should be fairly small as large specimens may eat other fishes. It is always better to have more than one fish of a species as they then act as a stimulus to each other and their colouring is shown off to best advantage. Another way to stock a community aquarium is with fishes of one species only. This can produce wonderful effects, especially with shoaling species.

It is very important not to overcrowd the aquarium as this leads to poor-looking fishes and a tendency towards disease. It is well to remember that fishes bought at pet shops are usually young and will grow larger in a tank.

When buying fishes the aquarist must choose healthy specimens and these must be transported home carefully. It is a good idea to make a small carrying case lined with expanded polystyrene in which the bag of fishes can be transported without loss of heat. For journeys of up to four hours the air above the water in the bag will be sufficient for the fishes, but for a longer journey the bag is better filled with oxygen. All large fish dealers will pack your fishes when a long journey home is involved. Once home the fishes must be carefully transferred to the tank, but preferably first to a quarantine tank.

They are best introduced by first floating the sealed bag in the aquarium to allow its temperature to adjust to that of the tank. The bag can then be opened and a small amount of tank water introduced. If no ill effects are apparent tank water can be introduced every half hour, until the water in the bag is nearly all tank water. The bag should then be allowed to sink in the tank and the fishes gently turned out. This prevents shock that might otherwise be caused by changes in $pH$, hardness, osmotic pressure and temperature. Once released the fishes should be given a small feed of some tempting live food to help introduce them to their new home.

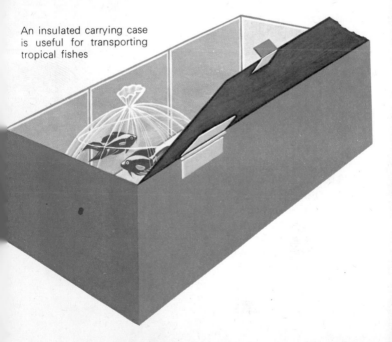

An insulated carrying case is useful for transporting tropical fishes

Sediment can be removed by siphon but the water must be replaced of course. The apparatus below removes debris without drawing off any water.

A tropical fish tank needs very little maintenance. Water evaporates and has to be replaced, theoretically with distilled water but in practice tap water will do. About once every month sufficient sediment will have collected on the gravel to spoil its clean appearance and this should be siphoned off using a siphon tube. A piece of clear polythene tube is useful for this, about ¾ inch in diameter. In running the siphon six gallons of water are usually taken out and replaced by fresh.

The only other occasional job for the aquarist is to scrape off the algae growing on the glass of his aquarium. Only the front glass needs to be cleaned regularly for algal growths on the back and sides can be beneficial. Algae are good oxygenators and prevent strong light entering

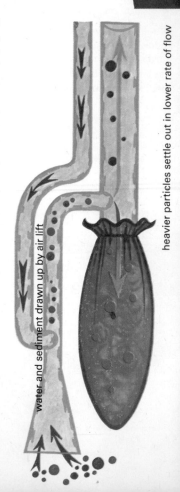

heavier particles settle out in lower rate of flow

water and sediment drawn up by air lift

the tank from the sides. Removal is easily done with a razor blade scraper though this job is done very effectively by the fish *Gyrinocheilus aymonieri,* one of which should be included in every community tank for this purpose.

Each day when feeding his fishes the aquarist should feel the temperature of the tank with the back of his fingers. In this way he will soon become experienced at estimating tank temperatures and this is very useful. Thermometers can go wrong, heaters can break and thermostats can stick, so a daily check on the temperature by thermometer and hand is a useful routine.

The only other danger, other than introducing diseased fishes or predators into the tank, is over-feeding. This danger cannot be stressed enough to the novice fish keeper. When the aquarist goes on holiday the fishes are much better left without feeding for up to three weeks in preference to having some novice fish keeper feeding them. The novice inevitably over-feeds, the excess food in the tank rots and causes a relative lack of oxygen which kills fishes.

*Gyrinocheilus aymonieri* is a useful aquarium fish. It cleans algae not only from aquarium glass but from the plants as well.

An attractive display of coral in a marine aquarium

## The tropical marine aquarium

A number of tropical freshwater aquarists graduate to keeping tropical marine aquaria. These are much more difficult to keep. The tank must be all glass or all plastic as sea water attacks metals releasing toxic metal ions, which will kill the fishes. Sea water is difficult to acquire unless one lives at the coast and even then it has to be taken from well out to sea to avoid pollution from rivers and sewage. Salts for preparing artificial sea water are now available, however. The tank must be equipped with efficient filtration and aeration systems. The loss of water by evaporation must be made up with distilled water and the density checked with a hydrometer. The bottom should be covered with washed silver sand and although there is no seaweed that will flourish in an aquarium, attractive displays can be made up with different varieties of corals and shells. Coral should be boiled before being placed in the aquarium.

Feeding can be a problem, as most coral fishes are carnivorous and will not take dried food. They can be fed *Daphnia*, *Tubifex,* Whiteworm and small freshwater fishes. None of these foods live long in salt water and therefore once dead must be quickly removed to prevent pollution. Adult Brine Shrimps are suitable but special arrangements have to be made to rear these to adult size.

## Tropical marine fishes

The Clown Anemone Fish *(Amphiprion percula)* is a native of the Indian Ocean and South East Asia. It has an interesting relationship with anemones of the genera *Stoichactis* and *Dicosoma*. The Clown Fishes are immune to the poisonous tentacles of the anemone among which they hide for protection.

The Pygmy Sea-horse *(Hippocampus zosterae)* is a fish in spite of its name and appearance. It has a prehensile tail and the male broods the eggs. Many of the public Aquaria have good displays of these or other species of sea-horses.

The Moorish Idol *(Zanclus canescens)* is probably the most coveted of all coral fishes but one of the most difficult to keep alive.

The Neon Goby *(Elacatinus oceanops)* is a very beautiful, active fish. It is noted for its habit of cleaning external parasites from other larger fishes.

The Emperor Angelfish *(Pomacanthus imperator)* is a hardy fish, but has a tendency to be aggressive with its own and similar species.

Clown Anemone Fish (1); Pygmy Sea-horse (2); Moorish Idol (3); Neon Goby (4); Emperor Angelfish (5)

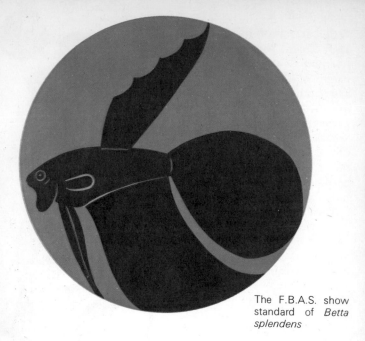

The F.B.A.S. show standard of *Betta splendens*

## Showing fishes

Fish shows may take the form of competitions between two or more fish clubs, or large open shows where fishes are entered by individuals from anywhere. The larger shows are usually well advertised in aquatic journals and are well worth a visit by the beginner as large numbers of excellent fishes are always on show.

In all large shows there is usually a furnished aquarium section. Here the competitor has to set up in a 24 × 12 × 12 inch tank a complete aquatic landscape and the judge usually gives marks under the following headings: design and character; fishes (selection, quality, condition); plants (selection, quality and condition) and technique. Then there are classes for individual fishes, often grouped into family classes, e.g., live-bearers; carps; barbs; minnows; cichlids; labyrinths and a final group for any other variety. Show standards have been laid down for certain fishes.

Standard methods of judging are also used, marks being given under five headings. Lists are published showing, for example, the size of swordtail that would gain twenty marks and the relative score for less full-grown ones. In allocation of marks for colour, fins, body shape, condition and deportment, the judge has to rely upon his experience. A recent development in Britain has been 'jar' shows where each exhibitor brings his fishes in a standard size sweet jar. This saves the organiser a great deal of trouble and money providing show tanks, and these 'jar table shows' have become very popular.

When entering for any show the rules should be scrutinized carefully, some rules varying from show to show. Getting a fish ready for a show involves initially picking out one's best fish in a likely class. About a month before the show this fish should be placed in a small aquarium devoid of plants, stones, gravel, etc., to get it used to being on its own. Small amounts of food should be fed frequently, getting the fish alert and used to humans. The fish should be exhibited in crystal clear water from its own tank and of course if it is a 'jar show' the jar should be clean both inside and out. Benching the fish as long as possible before the judging usually gives it time to settle down after its journey to the show.

Example of a judge's scoring card

No. of tank *12*

Specie of fish *Betta splendens*

| | Total marks possible | Marks awarded |
|---|---|---|
| Size.............................. | 20 | *14* |
| Colour............................ | 20 | *12* |
| Fins.............................. | 20 | *14* |
| Body shape........................ | 20 | *17* |
| Condition and deportment.......... | 20 | *14* |
| | 100 | *71* |

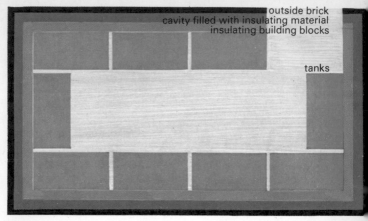

outside brick
cavity filled with insulating material
insulating building blocks

tanks

Floor and roof plan of a large, expensive, purpose-built fish house

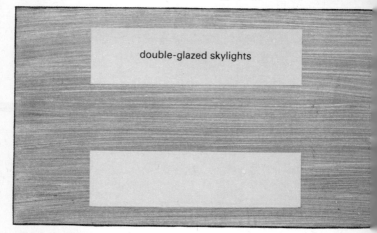

double-glazed skylights

## Fish houses and fish rooms

Many aquarists eventually get to the stage when they need a special place for their fish tanks. In the special fish house the design can be purely functional, bearing in mind the needs of the aquarist. If he wants to grow plants as well as fishes, for example, provision must be made for more natural light. Whether he decides to heat individual tanks or space heat the whole fish house will depend largely at what temperature he likes to work. Greenhouses on the whole make poor fish houses as they get too warm in summer, loose too much heat in winter and allow too much natural light to enter, causing overgrowth of algae.

In the more common type of fish house where tanks line one or more walls but the room contains relaxing chairs, etc., the design can obviously not be as functional. Whatever the type of aquarium accommodation, conservation of heat by double-glazing of windows, building with insulating blocks, cavity walls filled with polyurea foams, etc., are all very helpful and are to be recommended.

## Aquarist societies

Aquarist societies exist at international, national and local levels and the local aquarist society is by far the most valuable. At each meeting there is usually a speaker from outside the club who gives a talk on his special subject, followed by discussion. Local clubs also hold table shows either between club members or from time to time with other local clubs. In addition to these activities there is the opportunity of meeting and talking with other local aquarists. Clubs also organize outings to dealers and other places of aquatic interest.

Some of the larger clubs organize conventions, occasionally bringing distinguished speakers from other countries, and arranging large open shows. National organizations in Britain include the Federation of British Aquarist Societies (F.B.A.S.); and the British Aquarist Study Society (B.A.S.S.). The latter is a national organization with a limited membership of highly experienced aquarists devoted to research on aquatic subjects. These larger groupings set up guide-lines for the conduct of shows, perhaps have panels of speakers and

Aquarist society badges

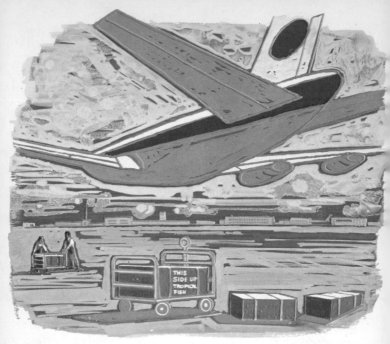

judges, set up standards for fishes and for judging and run large open shows.

In other countries organization is different in that there is one large national organization with a Central Committee of which local societies are all branches.

## Fish collection

Many fishes which cannot be easily bred in the aquarium are collected in the wild. Of course, collectors are also always on the look out for new species. Once the fishes are caught, transportation is often difficult, especially if the collector has had to go far into the bush to find his specimens. On arrival at his base the fishes are inspected and sorted and great care is taken with them by the collector until they are sold to a dealer – the second stage of their journey to our tanks. Finally they are put into plastic bags which are then blown up with oxygen, placed in insulated boxes and flown to their destination. They are collected by dealers on arrival and placed in quarantine tanks before resale to aquarists.

## Pet shops and fish dealers

Pet shops and dealers become very important to the aquarist and each soon has his favourite shop. Most towns have a local pet shop which keeps and sells all sorts of pets and pet foods and has anything from two to a hundred tanks of tropical fishes. This type of pet shop usually stocks all aquarium equipment and foods. Such local shops often tend to be a meeting place for local aquarists who are found standing round talking, if not actually buying. This type of shop buys fishes from wholesalers or from local aquarists whenever they have surplus stock.

The commercial fish breeder, often with large fish houses, breeds many varieties himself and often imports fishes from the tropics or from importers in Germany or Holland. Many of these dealers are naturally aquarists with great experience of fish breeding and fish keeping. Many of them sell both wholesale and retail.

Individual aquarists or aquarist societies are welcome by appointment at many of these establishments. In other countries where the weather is warmer, large commercial fish farms exist where the breeding and rearing of large numbers of tropical fishes takes place in outdoor pools and tanks.

Large fish farm in southern U.S.A.

# BOOKS TO READ

The following books are recommended for further general reading and are usually obtainable from bookshops and public libraries.

*All about Tropical Fish* by D. McInerny and G. Gerrard. Harrap, London, 1966.

*Encyclopedia of Tropical Fishes* by H. R. Axelrod and W. Vorderwinkler. Ward Lock, London, 1963.

*Exotic Tropical Fishes* by H. R. Axelrod. Bailey Bros., 1962.

*Freshwater Fishes of the World* by G. Sterba. (English Edition) Studio Vista, London, 1964.

*Freshwater Tropical Aquarium Fishes* by G. F. Hervey and J. Hems. Spring Books, London, 1965.

*Tropical Fish* by D. Gohm. Hamlyn, London, 1970.

*Tropical Aquarium Fishes – Freshwater and Marine* by G. Cust and G. Cox. Hamlyn, London, 1972.

In addition, the following are the three most popular aquarist journals in Britain and are available from most pet shops.

*The Aquarist and Pondkeeper*
*Pet Fish Monthly*
*Tropical Fish Hobbyist*


# PLACES TO VISIT

Listed here are a few recommended public Aquaria. Displays of tropical fishes can also be seen at most large zoos.

In Britain
Chester Zoo
Belle Vue Zoo, Manchester
Tower Aquarium, Blackpool
Brighton Aquarium
London Zoo Aquarium
Marineland, Morecambe

In U.S.A.
Bronx Zoo Aquarium, New York
Steinhart Aquarium, San Francisco
National Aquarium, Washington

In Australia
Taronga Zoological Park, Sydney

# INDEX

# TITLES IN THIS SERIES

**Arts & Collecting**
Art Nouveau for Collectors/Collecting and Looking After Antiques/
Collecting Inexpensive Antiques/Silver for Collectors/Toys & Dolls
for Collectors

**Domestic Animals and Pets**
Cats/Dog Care/Dogs/Horses and Ponies/Tropical Freshwater
Aquaria/Tropical Marine Aquaria

**Gardening**
Flower Arranging/Garden Flowers/Garden Shrubs/House Plants

**General Information**
Aircraft/Beachcombing and Beachcraft/Espionage/Freshwater
Fishing/Modern Combat Aircraft/Modern First Aid/Sailing/Sea
Fishing/Trains/Wargames

**History and Mythology**
Witchcraft and Black Magic

**Natural History**
Bird Behaviour/Birds of Prey/Birdwatching/Butterflies/Fishes of
the World/Fossils and Fossil Collecting/A Guide to the Seashore/
Prehistoric Animals/Seabirds/Seashells/Trees of the World

**Popular Science**
Astronomy/Biology/Ecology/Economics/Electricity/Electronics/
Exploring the Planets/Geology/The Human Body/Psychology/
Rocks, Minerals and Crystals/The Weather Guide